Open Our Eyes Lord

Bible Study and Devotional book

By
Paul Damsma

Copyright © 2023 by Paul Damsma

Publishing all rights reserved worldwide.

All rights reserved as sole property of the author.

The author guarantees all content is original and does not infringe upon the legal rights of any other person or work.

No part of this book may be reproduced, stored in a retrieval system, or transmitted in any form or by any means, without expressed written permission of the author.

Edited by Lil Barcaski

Published by: GWN Publishing

www.GWNPublishing.com

Cover Design: Kristina Conatser

ISBN: 978-1-959608-41-7

DEDICATION

To my father, through the years we enjoyed together, it seemed many of our hoped, dreams, plans and ideals were as shrouded as the mystery of what God held for us in the future. Now that you are in heaven, I have two fathers looking down on me! In your own way you showed your strengths and struggles, and proved that we persevere, and that each day, we hope and pray, is the best to come!

TABLE OF CONTENTS

PART 4—WILLING

PART 5—WORSHIP

INTRODUCTION

J. MICHAEL FINLEY

"I can only imagine, what my eyes will see, when your face is before me."

(1 CORINTHIANS 13: 12 - NIV - THOMAS NELSON)

"For now, we see only a reflection as in a mirror; then we shall see face to face. Now I know in part; then I shall know fully, even as I am fully known."

As author, it is not my wish to put ideas in the mind of the reader with this and future books, so I decided to change how the reader participates with this material.

I expect that if you are ready to read this book, you have belief in God, but thirst to know Him and His purpose for you at a deeper level. My concept is to provide a basepoint for those who wish to go further.

As an author, it is not my wish to put ideas in the mind of the reader with this and future books, so I want to place the onus on the reader to put the effort into reading the passages contained in every part and page so that they may reflect/meditate on these and grow in an understanding as the Spirit of God leads them forward.

Those wishing to express criticism that this way of presenting these concepts allows people to form opinions contrary to the author's ideals will be met with a shrug! I believe that the same Spirit of God who led 44 people to write the 66 books of the Bible, is the same Spirit that led the First Council of Constantinople to canonize the books of the Bible, and the same Spirit is responsible for the growth of the modern-day church, so their point is moot!

Adam and Eve's eyes were opened to knowledge of good and evil once they ate the fruit Satan tempted them with. Now we shall taste some of the tree of life and see once again that the Lord and His Word are good. Once this book opens your eyes a little, you will ask God to open them more each day. Amen!

How to use this book

This book is divided into five parts:

- God longs to lift us from darkness, bless, heal, bestow favor!
- We're reconnected, reconciled, aware we're Spirits, family!
- We commit to abide, to learn to be children, to live in love
- We align our will, lives, show love, power, and authority
- We devote our life to worship; we too change hearts and lives

Each part has 4 chapters

Each chapter has 10 letters (A through J)

Each letter will include:

- Required Bible passage readings (You're encouraged to write down things as the Spirit reveals them to you from the reading of the passage)
- A unifying passage of scripture that ties things together
- A relatable and fitting prayer which concludes the letter
- Chapters which are added for those wishing to read more

The reader should be forewarned, this book will require:

- Reflection and input by you; after all this book is written for your benefit, not mine.
- Ample time for studies and reflection.

PART 1

IMMUNITY

Freedom & Healing

JEREMIAH 17: 14

Heal me, Lord, and I will be healed; save me and I will be saved, for you are the one I praise.

Read Psalm 44: 2 – 4

Read Isaiah 1: 16 – 19

Read Romans 6: 18 – 23

Prayer

Thank you for cleansing us Lord and granting us a life like no other. Continue to expel threats, harm, and the evil others would mean to do to us. Make us a people of love, compassion and hope that others will want to know. May your holiness be demonstrated so no one doubts the peace, joy, and love that lives in us can only come from you. This we ask in Jesus name, Amen.

FOR DEEPER STUDY:

Psalm 44 • Isaiah 1 • Jeremiah 17 • Romans 6

CHAPTER 1

FAITH

(Your word is truth)

John 8: 32 – 36 • John 17: 13 – 19 • James 1: 13 – 18

There was a time when we searched for answers, with research, employing mathematical equations, theories, and empirical data that could be repeated ad nauseam, bringing us to the same conclusion with biology, ecology, astronomy, zoology, and technology.

Today, we have thousands of sooth-sayers, pedaling solutions for profit, and leading many astray. Governmental leaders act in their own interests, hurting the very people who vote for them and exposing them to dangers while further eroding faith in God. Now humanity lives in darkness, happy to spread it so people don't discover the truth.

JOHN 8: 32 - 36

And you shall know the truth, and the truth shall make you free." They answered Him, "We are Abraham's descendants, and have never been in bondage to anyone. How can You say, 'You will be made free'?" Jesus answered them, "Most assuredly, I say to you, whoever commits sin is a slave of sin. And a slave does not abide in the house forever, but a son abides forever. Therefore if the Son makes you free, you shall be free indeed.

But the truth is both convicting and freeing, and we suffer for lack! The world longs to be set free, but so long as they do not see Jesus freely living through us, they remain in hiding. The internet does this all to well, it must be a physical contact, showing love, compassion, and faith in Christ.

A. Believing Comes from Hearing

Read John 17: 1 – 5

Read Romans 1: 1 – 5

Read Ephesians 1: 18 – 20

> ROMANS 10: 18
>
> *But I say, have they not heard? Yes indeed: "Their sound has gone out to all the earth, And their words to the ends of the world."*

Prayer

Father, may our hearts long to know you more and more, open our eyes to the hearing of your words, whether from a pulpit, the speakers of our phones, computers, or autos, or when we speak them as we read! May we speak them over ourselves, our families, friends, neighbors, co-workers, communities and leaders. May the words of king David ring true: "Let the words of my mouth, and the meditations of my heart be acceptable in your sight, O Lord, my strength and my Redeemer." Amen.

FOR DEEPER STUDY:

John 17 • Romans 1 • Ephesians 1 – 6

B. Choose This Day

Read Joshua 24: 14 – 16

Read 2 Chronicles 34: 29 – 31

Read Matthew 11: 25 – 30

> DEUTERONOMY 30: 19
>
> *I call heaven and earth as witnesses today against you, that I have set before you life and death, blessing and cursing; therefore, choose life, that both you and your descendants may live.*

Prayer

Father, may our hearts believe your promises to the Israelites and all who have inherited the promises to Abraham. May we be courageous, as you commanded Joshua to be, and may all who see ask why we appear so hopeful amidst trouble, and unrest May the Lord make His face shine us, and be gracious to us as we live each and every day. May feel God the Father close to us, and let us turn from wrong doing, so that we may commune with Him once again. Amen!

FOR DEEPER STUDY:

Joshua 24: 14 – 24 • 2 Chronicles 34

C. These Were Written

Read John 20: 30 – 31

Read 1 Corinthians 10: 11 – 17

Read 1 John 2: 12 – 14

JAMES 3: 17

But the wisdom that comes from heaven, is first of all pure; then peace-loving, considerate, submissive, full of mercy and good fruit, impartial and sincere.

Prayer

Father, may our hearts grow more in step with you as we read your word, believing that you were able to do this. Your son did many more things than were recorded, but there is enough for us to see your plans in action, to save mankind, and bring us once again back to relationship with an eternal and loving God! May we meditate, now and forevermore, on your word, (which is truth) and be lifted so that we can transfix our eyes on you and your world. In Jesus's name we ask, Amen!

FOR DEEPER STUDY:

1 Corinthians 10 • 1 John 2

D. Giving God His Due

Read Psalm 33: 10 – 15

Read 1 Peter 2: 21 – 24

Read 1 Peter 4: 13 – 17

> 1 PETER 3: 15
>
> *But in your hearts revere Christ as Lord. Always be prepared to give an answer to everyone who asks you to give the reason for the hope that you have. But do this with gentleness and respect.*

Prayer

O God of heaven and earth, we thank you. Though the earth rumble and shake, you stand firm, your plans no man or government can stop. Jesus humbled himself, taking upon himself, one time the sins of man. May we, like Jesus, entrust ourselves to this power that we may do great things for you. And may He strengthen us, and give us grace and peace to stand when the world shows us hatred, so we might show the love of Jesus shines brighter than all things. Amen.

FOR DEEPER STUDY:

Psalm 33 • Joshua 1 • 1 Peter 2 – 4

E. Tested in the Truth

Read Psalm 66: 8 – 12

Read 1 Peter 1: 6 – 9

Read Romans 6: 1 – 3

HEBREWS 11: 16

But now they desire a better, that is, a heavenly country. Therefore God is not ashamed to be called their God, for He has prepared a city for them.

Prayer

O God of heaven and earth, when we are broken, we question the process instead of trusting our maker. May we learn to trust your perfect will, your tests, and seek to know your will. Only then will we see the perfection the posser makes of this broken pottery when His work is fully completed and perfected. May we stand on the firmness of your truth and authority, and may the light of life shine upon us. Amen.

FOR DEEPER STUDY:

Psalm 66 • 1 Peter 1 • Romans 6

F. Ask Seek & Knock in Faith

Read Luke 8: 22 – 25

Read James 1: 2 – 8

Read Hebrews 11: 1 – 6

HEBREWS 11: 6

And without faith it is impossible to please God, because anyone who comes to him must believe that he exists and that he rewards those who earnestly seek him.

Prayer

May we crave a faith that asks for you to move among your people in ways that renew hearts, minds, and lives. We know that the decision to follow Jesus has challenged families and friendships, and we call for you God to do this work because we believe that is exactly what you did for Abram. Your test of him on mount Moriah, cuts us to the bone, but your provision of a ram shows you provide a way as well as a sacrifice. May we too feed 5,000 with sustenance and the joy of fellowship that comes with knowing you. In Jesus name, Amen.

FOR DEEPER STUDY:

Luke 8 • James 1 – 5 • Hebrews 11, 12

G. Partaking in Fellowship

Read Hebrews 3: 12 – 14

Read 1 Corinthians 15: 33 – 38

Read 1 Thessalonians 4: 13 – 15

HEBREWS 11: 6

And without faith it is impossible to please God, because anyone who comes to him must believe that he exists and that he rewards those who earnestly seek him.

Prayer

Joyous communion, prayer, and praise unending, and the hope of life to come. In these, we rejoice, and thank God whose Spirit has given us the gifts to build His church and bring others into a loving relationship with him and one another. We have faith that you are working "all things for good for those that love you." Give us divine appointments and drive our hearts and minds to do your will, showing all that this life we live, is better when it is lived for you. In Jesus name, Amen.

FOR DEEPER STUDY:

Hebrews • 1 Corinthians 15 • 1 Thessalonians 4

H. Proclaiming Triumphantly

Read Isaiah 40: 1 – 5

Read Luke 12: 1 – 5

Read Acts 4: 8 – 13

ROMANS 16: 25

Now, to him who is able to establish you in accordance with my gospel, the message I proclaim about Jesus Christ, in keeping with the revelation of the mystery hidden for long ages past.

Prayer

Love immeasurable, forgiveness for sins, adoption as sons and daughters, and an eternal celebration of death to life. What an exciting calling to present this alternative to a world full of hurt, selfishness, greed, and corruption We have this everlasting gift within. We are a living Bible! Our actions and words need to show He is alive and living in us! This is part of the Greatest Commandment AND The Great Commission. As we speak, His Spirit convicts the hearts of people and this is an expression of answered prayer and a response to our faith. Amen.

FOR DEEPER STUDY:

Isaiah 40 • Luke 12 • Acts 4: 1 – 31

I . Death to Life

Read Romans 6: 8 – 12

Read Romans 8: 7 – 11

Read 2 Corinthians 7 – 11

ROMANS 8: 13

For if you live according to the flesh, you will die; but if by the Spirit you put to death the misdeeds of the body, you will live.

Prayer

Lord of life, give us eyes to see that a life in the Spirit carries us where our soiled sinful flesh cannot. Joyous communion, prayer and praise unending, and the hope of life to come. In these, we rejoice, and thank God whose Spirit has given us the gifts to build His church and bring others into a loving relationship with him and one another. Like the life we live, these lessons are hard, but we have faith that you are working "all things for good for those that love you." Give us your will, showing all that this life we live, is better when it is lived for you. In Jesus name, Amen.

FOR DEEPER STUDY:

Romans 6 – 8 • 2 Corinthians 7

J. Shine the Light

Read Matthew 5: 14 – 16

Read 2 Corinthians 4: 5 – 7

Read Ephesians 5: 8 – 14

JOHN 3: 21

Whoever lives by the truth comes into the light, so that it may be plainly seen that what they have done has been done in the sight of God.

Prayer

May we shine it brightly so that all who stumble in the dark may see it and be thankful for a way forward, and something in which to place their hope. May we attract people of all stripes, and backgrounds as we continue to shine it all the more on what you have done for us! May people come from near and far to see and hear what you have done and will do. As we continue to shine it, may all see the misdeeds and filthy rags they hold tightly to, and throw these away in favor of the rich robes you offer. Amen.

FOR DEEPER STUDY:

Matthew 5, 6 • 2 Corinthians 4, 5 • Ephesians 5, 6

CHAPTER 2

FLAWLESS

(Bloods Atoning)

Exodus 30: 7 – 10 • Hebrews 5: 5 – 10 • Hebrews 10: 11 – 14

The institutions of man, whether educational, healing, political, religious or employment related, always require one to do more, and achieve, so they may prove themselves. But systems of measurement are always changing and challenged. God says there is not one faithful, No, not one. So, He sent his son to do for us what we were unable to do for ourselves.

(HORACIUS BONAR, 1860'S)

"Not what my hands have done can save my guilty soul, not all my toiling flesh has born, can make my Spirit whole, not what I feel or do can give me peace with God, not all my prayers and sighs and tears, can bear my awful load."

HEBREWS 10: 11 - 14

And every priest stands ministering daily and offering repeatedly the same sacrifices, which can never take away sins. But this Man, after He had offered one sacrifice for sins forever, sat down at the right hand of God, from that time waiting till His enemies are made His footstool. For by one offering He has perfected forever those who are being sanctified.

This was his plan from the beginning, Even the tree of knowledge of good and evil was placed in the garden, not to diminish our God, but to give mankind a will. We chose poorly, but now, instead of every generation paying for Adam and Eve's discrepancy, and ensuing sinfulness, each of us can again choose!

A. Bloody Judgment

Read Genesis 4: 8 – 12

Psalm 9: 10 – 12

Isaiah 5: 7 – 9

> 1 JOHN 1: 7
>
> *But if we walk in the light as he is in the light, we have fellowship with one another, and the blood of Jesus Christ His Son cleanses us from all sin.*

Prayer

Father, let us endeavor to be our brother's and sister's keepers. For your call in Deuteronomy with the ten commandments and Jesus' greatest commandment to love. Let our conduct be to bless, to have compassion, and teach truth giving account for the blood you spilled when Jesus died on the cross. Give us reasons to work for good, in accordance with your will and good pleasure. Let us rejoice that You are a God who sees all and rewards people according to their deeds; may we humble ourselves in light of this. Grant that we give people, a place, a purpose, and an identity when this world seeks to take everything away, showing ourselves to be your disciples, shining a light on the path to righteousness.

FOR DEEPER STUDY:

Genesis 4 • Psalm 9 • Isaiah 5 • 1 John 1

B. Sacrificed & Outcast

Read Leviticus 16: 26 – 28

Read Matthew 27: 21 – 25

Read Galatians 3: 10 – 14

MARK 15: 34

And at the ninth hour Jesus cried out with a loud voice, saying, "Eloi Eloi lama sabactani?" which is translated, "My God, My God, why have you forsaken me?"

Prayer

Father, I'm forgiven, because Jesus was forsaken, I'm accepted, he was condemned I'm alive and well, your spirit is within me because he died and rose again Amazing Love, how can it be That you my king would die for me Amazing Love, I know it's true It's my joy to honor you, in all I do, I honor you. (Amazing Love by Chris Tomlin) They released a murderer in Jesus's place, and on the cross, he was crucified between two criminals, but he did no wrong. Jesus was obedient even to death on a cross, and the condemnation of man was put on Him. Forsaken, cursed, and cast out, that we maybe accepted. Amen!

FOR DEEPER STUDY:

Leviticus 16 • Matthew 27 • Mark 15 • Galatians 3

C. Perfect Sacrifice & Atonement

Read Leviticus 17: 10 – 12

Read Matthew 27: 24 – 26

Read Hebrews 9: 11 – 15

> ROMANS 8: 3
>
> *For what the law could not do in that it was weak through the flesh, God did by sending His own Son in the likeness of sinful flesh, on account of sin: He condemned sin in the flesh.*

Prayer

Father, we thank you for the blood that flows through our veins and capillaries. As the Pharisees said, let his blood be on us and our children. They didn't know that they were pleading his blood to cover their sins. Thank you for this one-time atoning sacrifice for all the sins of mankind. Once more, the gift of everlasting life is available to us who believe. Give us joy in the knowledge that we are saved, he was perfect, and sin was defeated, the law was satisfied, and the debt paid one time. Grant us a heart that longs to know our redeemer ever more each day, and an obedience to keeping your law and our purity. Amen.

FOR DEEPER STUDY:

Leviticus 17 • Matthew 27 • Romans 8 • Hebrews 9

D. Free Gifts of Grace, Favor, & Presence

Read Exodus 33: 12 – 14

Read Romans 5: 17 – 19

Read Ephesians 2: 8 – 10

> 2 CORINTHIANS 9: 8
>
> *And God is able to make all grace abound toward you, always having all sufficiency in all things, may have an abundance in every good work.*

Prayer

Grace, mercy, and peace from God the Father and from Jesus Christ, the Father's Son, will be with us in grace and truth. This comfort will be visible just as the pillar of smoke during the day and pillar of fire were at night for 40 years that the Israelites journeyed in the wilderness. Our sins separated us from you, but Jesus Death and resurrection have once again reconciled us to you, and never again will we be alone, never again will we wander away, for we long to be where you go. Thank you that this gift cannot be earned, you give it freely because you have work prepared for us to do, now and forever, Amen.

FOR DEEPER STUDY:

Exodus 33 • Romans 5 • 2 Corinthians 9 • Ephesians 2

E. All Realms Impacted

Read Luke 23: 39 – 43

Read Matthew 27: 45 – 52

Read Ephesians 4: 7 – 9

> ROMANS 16: 20
>
> *And the God of Peace will crush Satan under your feet shortly. The grace of our Lord Jesus Christ be with you, amen.*

Prayer

Father there isn't a multiverse that can compare, your story has it all, redemption, reconciliation, heaven, earth, and hell were not only mentioned, but equally impacted by Jesus' death and resurrection. Even more so, the criminals who were crucified with him contemplated their folly, and their end. One was forgiven and granted eternal life. Grant us hearts of wisdom to understand who you took captive, and what gifts we have received and how we should use them to give glory and thanks to you! Let your grace shower us and be evident to all, and let us see with our eyes Satan's end. In Jesus' name, Amen.

FOR DEEPER STUDY:

Luke 23 • Matthew 27 • Romans 16 • Ephesians 4

F. Reconciled

Read Romans 5: 9 – 11

Read 2 Corinthians 5: 18 – 20

Read Colossians 1: 21 – 23

ROMANS 6: 6

For we know that our old self was crucified with him so that the body ruled by sin might be done away with, that we should no longer be slaves to sin.

Prayer

Thank you for saving us from the eternal damnation we deserve, giving us a body of spirit and eternal life! Reconciliation was only possible through the death and resurrection of your son Jesus. May you use us to show the world that this loving gift was your plan from the beginning. Let all see that the tests we face are to change us into the sons and daughters you have destined us to be! Let us see ourselves as sons and daughters of a living and loving God, and let us bind ourselves as servants eternally to you, to love.

FOR DEEPER STUDY:

Romans 5, 6 • 2 Corinthians 4 – 6 • Colossians 1

G. Purified

Read Acts 15: 8 – 10

Read Hebrews 9: 22 – 24

Read 1 Peter 1: 21 – 23

HEBREWS 9: 28

So, Christ was sacrificed once to take away the sins of many; and he will appear a second time, not to bear sin, but to bring salvation to those who are waiting for him.

Prayer

The heart is inherently evil, God you know this, which is why you sent your son to teach a better way, and purify us, presenting us to you as blameless in your sight! My sinful heart cannot fathom this, but it gives immense joy and hope. The law of the Old Testament required that everything in the earth be covered by blood. The blood of Jesus covers everything in Earth and Heaven, including us, making all things right. Your promised Holy Spirit guarantees us passage to eternity! Amen.

FOR DEEPER STUDY:

Acts 15 • Hebrews 9 – 10 • 1 Peter 1

H. Restored

Read Psalms 51: 11 – 13

Read Psalm 103: 4 – 6

Read Romans 12: 1 – 3

GALATIANS 4: 7

So, you are no longer a slave, but God's child; and since you are his child, God has made you also an heir.

Prayer

Thank you, Father, for your restoration work. While many of us will be changed in the twinkling of the eye, our minds require more work than your Spirit. Be not angry and impatient, but help us to see this process as a gloriously great change. The graceless world in which we live cares not to give up what little control we have. Let us surrender in thanks to a gracious and merciful God. My chains are gone, I've been set free! Hallelujah, Amen!

FOR DEEPER STUDY:

Psalm 51 • Psalm 103 • Romans 12

I. Sealed

Read Ephesians 1: 11 – 14

Read Ephesians 4: 29 – 32

Read Revelation 7: 2 – 4

PSALM 139: 4 - 6

You hem me in behind and before,
and you lay your hand upon me.

Prayer

In a world where the rich believe in hedge funds, and schemes that allow profits were others are harmed, we have your hand around us. Satan claimed you hedged in Job and all he owned, so too you hold your peoples in your hand! Were predestined, working everything in our world into conformity with your will, putting hope in you, and filled with your Spirit. Nothing else is getting in or out. Grant us willing hearts to work to strengthen one another, with the help of your Spirit, so that nothing will stop your work, until it is completed, and you return to take us home to live with you, having shared with all the gospel message, and preaching salvation for every heart that believes.

FOR DEEPER STUDY:

Psalm 139 • Ephesians 1, 4 • Revelation 7

J. Overcomer

Read 1 John 2: 12 – 14

Read 1 John 5: 4 – 6

Read Revelation 12: 10 – 12

HEBREWS 11: 29

By faith, they passed through the Red Sea as by dry land, whereas the Egyptians, attempting to do so, were drowned.

Prayer

Thank you, Father for your Christ, and the obedient nature, that though he wanted to let the cup pass from him, endured the sin and shame of mankind and died on the cross. He overcame sin, death, Satan, and Hell. Jesus, when he sent out the 72, said he saw Satan fall like lightening from heaven. Jesus not only was raised from the dead, but he ascended to heaven, and is seated at God's right hand.

By believing, we too will see miracles done through Jesus' name, by the hand of God. Have faith, and believe, you too will overcome! Amen.

FOR DEEPER STUDY:

1 John 1 – 5 • Revelation 12 • Hebrews 11

CHAPTER 3

ACQUITTED

(Bloods atoning)

Zechariah 3: 1 – 3 • Romans 8: 1 – 3 • Revelation 12: 10 – 12

To say Satan was jealous of the creation of mankind was an understatement. he is threatening to undo us, driving a wedge between us, increasing sin in the world to bring on the new world order.

But God sent His Son Jesus, and changed everything in the blink of an eye! 40 days Jesus was alone in the wilderness while tempted by he Devil, and quoted the scriptures making the devil flee away, and bother him no more. Jesus death and resurrection opened the gates of heaven to and made us His Children again.

REVELATION 12: 10 - 12

Then I heard a loud voice in heaven say: "Now have come the salvation and the power and the kingdom of our God, and the authority of his Messiah. For the accuser of our brothers and sisters, who accuses them before our God day and night, has been hurled down. They triumphed over him by the blood of the Lamb and by the word of their testimony; they did not love their lives so much as to shrink from death. Therefore rejoice, you heavens and you who dwell in them! But woe to the earth and the sea, because the devil has gone down to you! He is filled with fury, because he knows that his time is short."

We use Spiritual tools like the Blood of Jesus and the word of our testimony to triumph over Evil and Satan. He continues to accuse, because that the only weapon at the Devils disposal, but we can rejoice that we have been forgiven!

A. Deceived

Read Genesis 3: 12 – 14

Read Luke 21: 7 – 9

Read Titus 3: 1 – 5

2 CORINTHIANS 1: 12

Now this is our boast: Our conscience testifies that we have conducted ourselves in the world, and especially in our relations with you, with integrity and Godly sincerity; we have done so, relying not on the world's wisdom, but God's grace.

Prayer

Father, we know that Satan lost his place in heaven and was sent to earth, but we did not understand his place, and gave him control. Grant us a Spirit that wills to take that power back by giving you the central place in our lives, instead of all the things on earth with which he can deceive us. Teach us to number our days right that we may develop a heart of wisdom, and a thirst for your word, and a passion to do your work. Many in our world deceive, and we bring the truth, make our words and deeds outshine the deceivers. This isn't easy work, but you go with us. Amen.

FOR DEEPER STUDY:

Genesis 3 • Luke 21 • 2 Corinthians 1 • Titus 3

B. Confirmed

Read Luke 3: 21 – 23

Read John 14: 5 – 5

Read Galatians 3: 26 – 29

EPHESIANS 1: 7

In Him we have redemption through His blood, the forgiveness of sins, according to the riches of His grace.

Prayer

Father in heaven, just as you approved of the words and works of your son Jesus, so too, because of His sacrifice and work in our lives, we too are approved. We accept baptism, not just for forgiveness of sin, but also for the laying on of hands and receipt of your Holy Spirit, who guides us in all righteousness and tells us what you want us to do. Even when we do not know the way, you guide and lead us in your righteousness. Thank you for making this possible because we could never do it on our own. Amen.

FOR DEEPER STUDY:

Luke 3, 4 • John 14 • Galatians 3

C. Cursed

Read Genesis 3: 17 – 19

Read Jeremiah 17: 4 – 6

Read Galatians 3: 12 – 14

EPHESIANS 1: 4

Just as He chose us in Him before the foundation of the world, that we should be holy and without blame before Him in love.

Prayer

Thank you, for having a plan that included me! Adam and Eve's sin was great, and the curse on the earth is depressing, and for some families heartbreaking and mind numbing, but you love every soul and all we have and are, we owe to you! The mind is inherently evil and who can know it, therefore you are right to tell us not to trust in man. Thank you for removing the curse, and replacing it with blessing. You chose me, and others and cleansed us from sin, so we may enter your throne blameless without fear. Only you could do this. Amen.

FOR DEEPER STUDY:

Genesis 3 • Jeremiah 17: 4 – 13 • Galatians 3

D. Tempted

Read Job 2: 8 – 10

Read Luke 4: 1 – 4

Read Hebrews 4: 14 – 16

> JAMES 1: 12
>
> *Blessed is the man who endures temptation; for when he has been approved, he will receive the crown of life which the Lord has promised to those who love Him.*

Prayer

Lord how I wish I had someone who explained this scripture when I was young, I may have better understood the life I live and what was happening! But through knowing, may I not yield to the tempter, nor allow myself to be fooled any longer, instead being a tool for your purposes and pleasure. Knowing that Jesus himself was tempted is helpful, however at times when our faith is compromised and our doubt grows.

FOR DEEPER STUDY:

Job 2 • Luke 4 • Hebrews 4 • James 1

E. Chosen

Read Exodus 9:14 – 17

Read Deuteronomy 7: 1 – 8

Read 1 Peter 2: 7 – 10

1 SAMUEL 16: 7

But the LORD said to Samuel, "Do not consider his appearance or his height, for I have rejected him. The LORD does not look at the things people look at. People look at the outward appearance, but the LORD looks at the heart."

Prayer

King David was right to ask, "What is man that you are mindful of him?" We are often selfish, impulsive, greedy, and hungry for power. May our eyes be opened to the very fine details you put into the saving and sanctifying and discipline of your people, that we may understand how the transforming work of the Spirit makes us into a people useful for the purposes for which you have chosen us. This we pray in the name of your Son Jesus, Amen.

FOR DEEPER STUDY:

Exodus 9 • Deuteronomy 7 • 1 Samuel 16 • 1 Peter 2

F. Our Savior & Lord

Read Matthew 27: 20 – 22

Read Ephesians 1: 2 – 4

Read Hebrews 7: 26 – 28

> ROMANS 8: 28
>
> *And we know that all things work together for good to those who love God, to those who are the called according to His purpose.*

Prayer

Lord our ways are not our ways, and no Hollywood Director will get this right unless you are producing the movie! We are also happy, as with creation that you have not made us robots to do your will without question, rather we were and are given a choice. At the end the world is still in need of a savior, and they do not know that it is Jesus. When we begin to understand that He had a plan for us from the beginning do we understand that we were meant to be a part of His family. We awake daily, eager to know your plans for us, and we ask you to make them unfold as we step out into your world, and make them happen. Amen.

FOR DEEPER STUDY:

27 • Romans 8 • Ephesians 1 • Hebrews 7

G. Accused

Read Zechariah 3: 1 – 4

Read Mark 15: 1 – 5

Read Revelation 12: 9 – 11

ZECHARIAH 3: 4

The angel said to those who were standing before him, "Take off his filthy clothes." Then he said to Joshua, "See, I have taken away your sin, and I will put fine garments on you."

Prayer

Oh Lord, you have silenced the accuser. Though he shouts from the halls of the courts of heaven as he did in the days of Job and Moses and Joshua and Jesus, the sacrifice of your Son was enough to satisfy the righteous requirements for the sins of each and every believer! In our place, he was accused for all the things for which mankind seek vengeance and blood. While we may shudder that he is with us on earth, we see that he maybe overcome! God, through His son Jesus showed us how this might be done. Amen

FOR DEEPER STUDY:

Zechariah 3 • Mark 15 • Revelation 12

H. Death & Hell Defeated

Read 1 Corinthians 15: 50 – 56

Read Ephesians 4: 7 - 10

Read Revelation 20: 4 – 6

HEBREWS 11: 16

But now they desire a better, that is, a heavenly country. Therefore God is not ashamed to be called their God, for He has prepared a city for them.

Prayer

Thank you God, for granting that we might live forever in your paradise, free from the influences of Satan and his fallen angels. We can leave behind the filth, the corruption the grief of loss, the devastation of disease, and the darkness of chaos and deceit and oppression. We pray against these now, and work to expose these while seeking to show a better solution; help us to show this world you and all you have done for us. I do not call people bad to their face, but ask that you judge them, but your word says after this life, we will judge with you. Let us live with a life worthy of that calling. Amen.

FOR DEEPER STUDY:

1 Corinthians 15 • Ephesians 4 • Hebrews 11

I. Overshadowed

Read Isaiah 9:1 – 3

Read Luke 1: 34 – 36

Read Mark 9: 5 – 8

MATTHEW 24: 36

But about that day or hour no one knows, not even the angels in heaven, nor the Son, but only the Father.

Prayer

Father, we often cry when disappointed, frustrated or depressed. Help us to refocus our energies to focus on what's happening under the shadow of the veil. Your son was beautiful in a manger, and grew up in humble surroundings, but was a King and Savior of mankind. You have hidden in us the giftings, opportunities and timing of your will to do wonderful things. May we daily ask that you carry these out so all may see the Light of life displayed in us. Thank you for sending Jesus as an example. Amen.

FOR DEEPER STUDY:

Isaiah 9: 1 – 7 • Luke 1 • Mark 9

J. Sanctified & Prized

Read Ephesians 1 – 3

Read Hebrews 2: 10 – 13

Read 1 John 3: 17 – 19

> 1 CORINTHIANS 6: 11
>
> *And that is what some of you were. But you were washed, you were sanctified, you were justified in the name of the Lord Jesus Christ and by the Spirit of our God.*

Prayer

Thank you for sending Jesus to this earth and giving us an example to follow. We know that purity is not easy, which is why you also provided a perfectly unblemished sacrifice, and raised him again to life. So too we know that our lives are a process of coming clean, and being presented that way to you at your Son's second coming to earth! We will put our trust in you and work to show others your ways, giving to each as they have need, showing by our actions that we love them. This is how we set our hearts at rest in Your presence. Amen Lord, so shall it be!

FOR DEEPER STUDY:

Ephesians 1, 2 • Hebrews 2 • 1 John 3

CHAPTER 4

HOLY

(Arms of Strength)

Leviticus 19: 1 - 4 • Numbers 11: 21 – 23 • John 17: 10 - 12

YouTube videos shows technological advances in the United States air force, navy, and armed forces. Every year Moscow showcases their stockpiles, and young people are persuaded to join the Red Army. Many have perished over the last year in the war with Ukraine.

God commanded obedience, and purity too. This idea of putting God first is echoed throughout the scriptures. "Seek first His kingdom and righteousness." "If you treat as Holy, My Sabbath." Idolatry is forbidden. God fed all the people in the wilderness, their sandals did not wear out for 40 years, but not one of the elders saw the promised land. Moses saw it from a distance.

But there is an enemy and power that is unseen, and many feel its presence but are powerless to stop it. Some things are clear enough. The Philistines had Goliath, but the Babylonians spread out over the land like a swarm of locusts, devouring everything in their path. The Roman Praetorian Guards were menacing, and the Israelites disliked them, but they also feared them.

JOHN 17: 10 - 12

All I have is yours, and all you have is mine.And glory has come to me through them.I will remain in the world no longer, but they are still in the world, and I am coming to you.Holy Father, protect them by the power ofyour name, the name you gave me, so that they may be oneas we are one. While I was with them, I protected them and kept them safe bythat name you gave me. None has been lostexcept the one doomed to destructionso that Scripture would befulfilled.

A. Wisdom & Gladness

Read Proverbs 3: 5 – 8

Read Matthew 7: 24 – 27

Read James 3: 16 – 18

PROVERBS 23: 16

Yes, my inmost being will rejoice
when your lips speak right things.

Prayer

Father, there is so much about this world of yours that is strange to us, and we cannot know your will for us unless we ask you, believing you are calling us forwards in faith, trusting that everything unfolds as it should! As one poplar hymn says, "I need thee every hour," we can't boast about what will happen tomorrow, but we can work to establish treasures in heaven, building on the rock that is Jesus. We speak your name with certainty, showing by all we do and say that your way is the only one that works, and everything else is sinking sand. Amen.

FOR DEEPER STUDY:

Proverbs 3, 23 • Matthew 7 • James 3

B. Making Plans, Seeking Direction, Trusting Him

Read Jeremiah 29: 10 – 12

Read Romans 8: 18 – 20

Rear Ephesians 1: 7 – 12

> JEREMIAH 29: 11
>
> *"For I know the plans I have for you," declares the Lord, "plans to prosper you and not to harm you, plans to give you hope and a future."*

Prayer

Father, we know that circumstances, perception, and unfortunate events occur that make us question our faith in ourselves and you. We pray that your Spirit may be there to calm our hearts and minds and remind us that you are still in control. James tells us not to waver in our belief when seeking your wisdom and direction, and you spoke through Paul about the events that will yet take place. The people in Ephesus, Philippi, and Rome were told You have had things planned from start to finish, so we are not to question why you made us but trust your processes and follow them knowing you are in the details. Amen.

FOR DEEPER STUDY:

Jeremiah 29 • Romans 8 • Ephesians 1 • Philippians 1

C. Gentle & Loving

Read 2 Samuel 22: 35 – 37

Read Psalm 143: 8 – 10

Read Matthew 11: 28 – 30

PROVERBS 4: 13

Take firm hold of instruction, do not let go; Keep her, for she is your life.

Prayer

Gentleness, loving kindness, peace and deliverance. These seem lofty, like the stars, unreachable for us, but only in your presence can we enjoy these. May we long for this each and every day, your gifts and your blessings and your miracles for your people. With man these things are impossible, but you can do all things. You correct us when we go down wrong paths, you hedge us in, you correct us, you show yourself when we turn our soul and mind to you, counting on you to help us keep the greatest commandment. We want power, but we want a crown that has no value, show us that our world is still worth living for and the people worth saving. Amen.

FOR DEEPER STUDY:

2 Samuel 22 • Psalm 143, 144 • Proverbs 4 • Matthew 11

D. Faithful & Joyful

Read Acts 8: 38 – 40

Read Romans 12: 14 – 16

Read Galatians 5: 22 – 24

REVELATION 4: 13

Then I heard a voice from heaven saying to me,
"Write: 'Blessed are the dead who die in the Lord from now on.' "
"Yes," says the Spirit, "that they may rest from their labors, and
their works follow them."

Prayer

Father there is joy in your presence, so never send me away from it. May we be intrepid to share the gospel, filled with joy to seeing wonderment in those who ask why were different. Philip changed the Eunich from Ethiopia, perhaps even that country. May He give us boldness to show by our word and action that were His brothers and sisters. May we labor for souls and not skimp on grace and love for all mankind. Like that day 2050 or so years ago, may we once again say, "joy to the world." Amen.

FOR DEEPER STUDY:

Acts 8 • Romans 12 • Galatians 5 • Revelation 4

E. Powerful & Zealous

Read Deuteronomy 7: 18 – 20

Read Psalm 98: 1 – 3

Read Ephesians 6: 9 – 11

> PHILIPPIANS 1: 6
>
> *Being confident of this very thing, that he who has begun a good work in you will complete it until the day of Christ Jesus.*

Prayer

Lord, we are forever thankful that you are on our side, because so many in our world wander about not knowing which side is the stronger, or even who you are, while others think themselves losers. We are on the winning side, and you proved it when you led the Israelites form captivity and drove out the nations in Canaan. Though they did not remove them completely, the conquests of David and the Wealth of Solomon are well documented. Like David, the Disciples saw Jesus command the wind and waves to be still! We need to have faith that you will show yourself to believers and unbelievers alike in the time to come, may your kingdom come. Amen.

FOR DEEPER STUDY:

Deuteronomy 7 • Psalm 98 • Ephesians 6

F. Equipped & Satisfied

Read Psalm 103: 1 – 5

Read 2 Timothy 3: 14 – 17

Read James 1: 16 – 18

PHILIPPIANS 4: 19

And my God will meet all your needs according to the riches of his glory in Christ Jesus.

Prayer

When I see the eagle soar through the air, I long for such strength and majesty! But to know that you are as near as the whisper of your name, you who gave us life, and breath, will also keep us safe and will shelter us during this lifetime. We need your forgiveness and peace, for your crown of loving kindness. May we rejoice in your words and trust your will for our lives. Even now, I find life difficult, but I know you have a plan, and that keeps me going. May your word teach, and convict me when necessary. In all our uncomfortable places and decisions, may we lean on your everlasting love. Hug us with those arms that hugged David when pursued and hated. Bring us back to life, and give us everything needed so we can show the world that you alone satisfy.

FOR DEEPER STUDY:

Psalm 103 • 2 Timothy 3 • James 1 • Philippians 4

G. Giving & Understanding

Read Joshua 21: 43 – 45

Read Daniel 6:23 – 25

Read Acts 27: 34 – 36

JEREMIAH 3: 15

And I will give you shepherds according to My heart, who willfeed you with knowledge and understanding.

Prayer

God, you love to shower us with blessings. Family, friends, possessions, occupations, habitations, functions, and enjoyment. Help us to see which are for our use, your glory, and our pleasure. Give us peace from enemies and a hedge of protection that they can see. Should we be in another country, or taken captive, let the leaders of that world see your hand upon everything we say and do. May you protect our families in the palm of your hands and provide us with the knowledge that there is noting you cannot do. May we too see that your will cannot be thwarted and may we never feel threatened in doing it. Give us wise and discerning friends to help guide and direct us in Jesus' name, Amen.

FOR DEEPER STUDY:

Joshua 21 • Daniel 1-6 • Acts 27 • Jeremiah 3

H. Discipled & Predestined

Read Romans 8: 28 – 32

Read Ephesians 1: 3 – 6

Read Hebrews 12: 7 – 9

PSALM 139: 16

Your eyes saw my unformed body; the days ordained for me were written in your book before one of them came to be.

Prayer

Every day the things happen that run us down, challenge our values, priorities and challenge who we are, but God is still in control. Let Him be glorified in how we live, so all may see that we are different and give glory to God. We will have visible scars, but He is making us better by the struggles and challenges. We are adopted as sons and daughters of God! Let the world see this mystery pay out, and they will know that we were chosen by God for specific tasks, showing His Spirit working through us. Amen.

FOR DEEPER STUDY:

Psalm 139 • Romans 8 • Ephesians 1 • Hebrews 12

I. Pure & Righteous

Read 2 Chronicles 16: 7 – 10

Read Isaiah 61: 1 – 3

Read Amos 4: 10 – 12

2 THESSALONIANS 1: 10 – 12

With this in mind, we constantly pray for you, that our God may make you worthy of his calling, and that by his power he may bring to fruition your every desire for goodness and your every deed prompted by faith.

Prayer

There is no one bigger, stronger, or swifter, or more protecting. Were sorry when our hearts and minds do not love you and our fellow man. When we do not acknowledge you in all our ways, we fail. Grant that your Spirit to ensure we do all that you need, and give us peace of mind that you are with us. Lord, we pray, continue to deliver our enemies into our hands, and let us commit them to your hands; to judge, to discipline, to make into your tool for good. Help us to remember what we are, and all that you have done for us in the name of reconciliation. Amen.

FOR DEEPER STUDY:

2 Chronicles 16 • Isaiah 61 • Amos 4 • 2 Thessalonians 1

J. Committed & Rooted

Read Colossians 2: 6 – 8

Read 1 Corinthians 3: 12 – 14

Read Ephesians 3: 14 – 21

PROVERBS 12: 3

A man is not established by wickedness, But the root of the righteous cannot be moved.

Prayer

Father, help us to believe (in faith) we will do all for God, as the apostle Paul says, Our struggle is not against flesh or blood; when squeezed, perplexed, in pain or feeling defeated, may we fall on His everlasting arms. May we ask, "What does it mean to love the Lord with all your heart, mind, soul, and strength?" May our every step, from here into eternity, and our every work reveal you and not the filthy rags we began with. May we thankfully bend the knee, remembering that we can do nothing apart from you. Fill our hearts, and ground us in you, in faith, eagerly seeking you daily, and your will for today and every day, Amen.

FOR DEEPER STUDY:

Colossians 2 • 1 Corinthians 3 • Ephesians 3

PART 2

RENEWED

(New Family, Heart & Spirit)

Genesis 5: 21 - 24 • Ezekiel 36: 25 – 27 • Colossians 3: 9-11

> 2 CORINTHIANS 4: 16
>
> *Therefore we do not lose heart. Though outwardly we are wasting away, yet inwardly we are being renewed day by day.*

Prayer

Father, many are intrigued by the story of Moses, who parted the waters, or Solomon who had wisdom and riches like no other ruler in the World. So too, we think of Enoch, who never tasted death, what a heart for you he must have had. May the waters of baptism remove every idol, and give us a heart that understands the Spiritual wisdom of you have for all. If our hearts beat now, may it bee you we breathe in and out, so that all may bee given life by your word, breathed into the lungs and hearts of all. Give us hearts full of love and grace and peace, so all may be welcomed to see that you are indeed enough. This we ask in Jesus' name, Amen.

FOR DEEPER STUDY:

Genesis 5 • Ezekiel 36 • 2 Corinthians 4 • Colossians 3

CHAPTER 5

RECONCILED

(It is finished)

John 5 • 2 Corinthians 5 • Hebrews 12

Day after day, we live in misery, feeling the stain of sin, the pain of shame, the weight of generations of sins, and the knowledge that we are dying a slow death. We long for a savior, someone to wash this sin and shame from our bodies, to break the chains of curses, wrongful agreements, and addictions, not knowing that one has done all this already!

The Israelites had leaders, judges, kings and prophets. Not only were books written about them, there were also books written by them, as the Spirit of God moved them! But Jesus promises that God will even raise some from the dead, and give them life. As children of God, you too are included in this. God is your leader, your savior, and your Father, He gives us all we need!

> 2 CORINTHIANS 5: 14 - 19
>
> *So from now on we regard no one from a worldly point of view. Though we once regarded Christ in this way, we do so no longer. Therefore, if anyone is in Christ, the new creation has come: The old has gone, the new is here! All this is from God, who reconciled us to himself through Christ and gave us the ministry of reconciliation: that God was reconciling the world to himself in Christ, not counting people's sins against them. And he has committed to us the message of reconciliation.*

So, I will echo Billy Graham and all the saints and evangelists of the past and ask you, who are you living for? Who does your heart beat for? You who have been recreated, rejoice, and be glad, because you have been given a new name, a new life, renewed energy and purpose. Don't, for a moment, take it for granted, and rejoice that you have been reconciled to God!

A. Betrayed & Established

Read Matthew 27: 1 – 4

Read Acts 7: 51 – 53

Read Hebrews 13: 7 – 9

PSALM 2: 8

Ask of Me and I will give you the nations for you the nations for your inheritance, and the ends of the earth for your possession.

Prayer

No plan of angel or man can thwart you or change your course, Lord. You are in complete control. It is true the religious leaders and even the soldiers of Rome treated you with contempt. A disciple of your 12 chose to betray you for 30 pieces of silver. Paul the apostle reminded the people that many people and leaders sought to end the prophets who spoke your words. May we be forever in awe, and unison, in agreeing to do your will and bring this light to a people living in darkness, despair, and hatred. We know that heaven and earth will pass away, but you and your word are firmly established as you have promised. Amen Lord.

FOR DEEPER STUDY:

Matthew 27 • Acts 7 • Hebrews 13 • Psalms 2

B. Forsaken & Accepted

Read Isaiah 56: 6 – 8

Read Matthew 26: 55 – 57

Read Matthew 27: 45 – 47

EPHESIANS 1: 7

In Him we have redemption through His blood, the forgiveness of sins, according to the riches of His grace.

Prayer

Thank you for sending your Son into the world, for we could never hope to accomplish all that you have done for us. Sacrifice and atonement were made were made together, and the perfect sacrifice didn't stay down, but opened the way for us to be made alive in Christ. This was foretold and was fulfilled when the time was right. May all be made Spiritually alive who love you and are moved to do your will. You were forsaken, we were accepted. Praise God, His plans no one can change. You redeemed us to yourself, You paid the ultimate price for our sin. May we truly seek to know the extent of your love for us, being lead in the Spirit to do all the things that bless others and glorify You. Amen.

FOR DEEPER STUDY:

Isaiah 56 • Matthew 26, 27 • Ephesians 1

C. Denied & Approved

Read Mark 14: 66 – 68

Read Mark 14: 69 – 72

Read 2 Timothy 2: 13 – 15

1 THESSALONIANS 2: 4

But as we have been approved by God to be entrusted with the gospel, even so we speak, not as pleasing men, but God who tests our hearts.

Prayer

Father, we are truly sorry when our words and behaviors have denied you and your son Jesus. Our sin has blinded us and made us selfish, plans, dreams, ambitions, and thoughts are driving a wedge between us and you, and so hurt those around us. Let us be deeply planted in you, watered by the Word of God, and providing evident and strengthening fruit for all to enjoy. Let us lose this fear and admit it, being proud that we are children of the living God! The cost of the cross is not cheap, so let us show the world that we are approved by you because Jesus was denied and went to the cross for us. Amazing grace, how sweet the sound! Amen.

FOR DEEPER STUDY:

Mark 14 • 2 Timothy 2 • Psalm 1

D. Judged & Purposed

Read John 6: 63 – 65

Read John 7: 21 – 24

Read John 15: 18 – 21

JEREMIAH 29: 11

For I know the thoughts I have towards you, says the Lord, thoughts of peace and not of evil, to give you a future and a hope.

Prayer

Father, we are truly sorry for our days of doubt and loathing, those days of laughing at your Son's claims of being one with you. May we pray for those whose doubt and disbelief continue to hurt you, us and others who do not yet know you. Jesus did miracles to bring hope to them that believe. May we, like him bring hope and peace to a disbelieving and hopeless world that suffers in chaos and darkness. You warned the apostles, and us that the world will hate us because it hated you, because you chose Him and us to serve. May we make it our life's work to make the world know you and the hope that you give to all who will call on you name and believe. Amen.

FOR DEEPER STUDY:

John 6, 7, 15 • Jeremiah 29

E. Condemned & Justified

Read Isaiah 53: 4 – 6

Read John 19: 5 – 7

Read Hebrews 2: 14 – 18

2 CORINTHIANS 5: 21

For He made Him who knew no sin to be sin for us, that we might become the righteousness of God in Him.

Prayer

Father, we thank you that you had this planned from the start. We understand that there was no other way but to send your only Begotten son into the world to live and die for us. We do not deserve this nor do we understand this level of love and commitment, but we are justified, and he was condemned to die on a cross. You said anyone who was hung on a cross was condemned, but you also raised him up, and seated Him next to you until all His enemies are put under foot. He also being human faced temptation, so He can identify, and intercede for us. Show us daily how to become more like you, and remind us of how we made all this possible, and lead us in the way everlasting. In Jesus name, Amen.

FOR DEEPER STUDY:

Isaiah 53 • John 19 • Hebrews 2 • 2 Corinthians 5

F. Crucified & Freed

Read Isaiah 53: 7 - 9

Read Matthew 27: 35 - 37

Read Galatians 2: 19 - 2

ROMANS 7: 6

But now we have been delivered from the law, having died to what we were held by, so that we should serve in the newness of the Spirit and not in the oldness of the letter.

Prayer

Lord, we know Jesus was both willing and overwhelmed when he prayed on the mountain of olives that this cup might pass him by. You spoke through the prophet Isaiah of how he was treated like a prisoner and nobody carried on his name. How he was crucified and died as a criminal, but was innocent. It should have been us, but you saw fir to let your own see death for our sin. But His death was the death of many things including sin, and the law. No sacrifice or scapegoat could do what He did for all mankind. We are delivered from the law, and from judgment. May we use that freedom to serve you and let others know of this freedom that gives all great joy, in Jesus' name, Amen.

FOR DEEPER STUDY:

Isaiah 53 • Matthew 27 • Galatians 2 • Romans 7

G. Stabbed & Healed

Read Luke 8: 42 – 44

Read John 19: 33 – 35

Read John 20: 26 – 28

> 1 PETER 2: 24
>
> *...who Himself bore our sins in His own body on the tree, that we, having died to sins, might live for righteousness—by whose stripes you were healed.*

Prayer

Thank you, Lord, for opening the disciple's eyes to the scriptures, during Jesus' life and ministry on earth, and after he arose. May we, through our trials, tribulation and even persecution, be healed of our filth, the stench of smoke, and be cleansed, so that we may be presented to you, pure and clean, and right at the return of Christ. Bless all who did not see Jesus rise, but believe. We ask that you would be willing to give us the world, if only to save the souls of all mankind, and show unbelievers that there is a better way to live in you! May each and every day be an opportunity to show our joy, gratitude and peace in you. Amen.

FOR DEEPER STUDY:

Luke 8 • John 19 - 20 • 1 Peter 2

H. Buried & Covered

Read Matthew 27: 24 – 26

Read Luke 23: 50 – 53

Read 2 Peter 1: 8 – 10

ROMANS 4: 6 – 8

Blessed are those whose lawless deeds are forgiven, and whose sins are covered;

Prayer

Oh Lord, we thank you for the outpouring of your Holy Spirit, but we also thank you for the outpouring of Jesus blood upon us and our world. As in the days of Moses, only the blood could atone for the sins of the people, and only the priests could slaughter and burn the sacrifices, and put the blood on the parts of the tabernacle and temple. Jesus was the perfect sacrifice, and he was buried in a linen shroud and laid in a cave. Grant to us Lord that we may blossom in the fruits of the faith and spirit, as we reach out to you and our fellow man. Fill us with these, so that all might reach out to take hold of you once again, instead of the tree of good and evil. These things we pray in Jesus' name, Amen.

FOR DEEPER STUDY:

Matthew 27 • Luke 23 • 2 Peter 1 • Romans 4

I. Descended & Consumed

Read Ephesians 4: 7 – 10

Read Acts 2: 26 – 28

Read Hebrews 12: 29

2 PETER 3: 11

Therefore, since all these things will be dissolved, what manner of persons ought you to be in holy conduct and godliness.

Prayer

Thank you, Father, for sending Jesus to hell with our sins, and granting us the gifts of your Spirit, that we might become your children! May we continue to grow in these and in love for you and one another. Jesus overcame Satan, sin, the law, and death, in one fell swoop, and we will be eternally grateful, because we could never do this on our own. Our hearts are filled with gratitude and joy that you did all that we could not. The body may die, but our spirit rests until you call us to rise, and see the end of this world and the rise of an eternal kingdom, ours to share with you. Such love is too much for me to fathom. Thank you, Amen.

FOR DEEPER STUDY:

Acts 2 • Ephesians 4 • Hebrews 12 • 2 Peter 3

J. Resurrected & Reconciled

Read Matthew 22: 29 – 33

Read Luke 24: 25 – 27

Read Ephesians 1: 19 – 21

2 CORINTHIANS 5: 21

For He made Him who knew no sin to be sin for us, that we might become the righteousness of God in Him.

Prayer

Father, we have heard so much of the Spirit, and yet we do not understand enough. We can identify with Nicodemus, who was a Pharisee, a leader of the people, but was amazed "what is this teaching that says we must be born again?" Jesus would set the tone, telling the people that a grain of wheat falls in the ground and dies so that the seed inside maybe sheltered till it is nourished by ground and water and pokes out of the ground. It was necessary for our Lord to do this as an example for us all. You once again allowed us to walk and talk to you, in the cool of the day, to wonder aloud (in prayer) and edify others, and intercede for others. Thank you for your loving example. Amen.

FOR DEEPER STUDY:

Matthew 22 • Luke 24 • John 3, 12 • Ephesians 1 • 2 Corinthians 5

CHAPTER 6

BEGOTTEN

(Children of God)

Isaiah 45 • Romans 8 • Titus 3

All through the Bible are stories of good and evil, oppression, and freedom, testing, laws and idolatry. If we see it only as that, it appears only to be a tug of war, but instead, we get the backstories and narrative of the major players, the ones who obey evil, and those who obey God. Some were judges, and leaders, others were prophets, still others kings.

Many today are pondering what Solomon (the earth's wisest man) pondered, why do we feel such a connection to things that move our soul? The fact is, we are much more than the physical man or woman people see. We are spirit! This is why we feel pain, emotion, connection, and a longing that this world and all it holds can never fill!

We are part of Abraham's family, and therefore, part of God's family! This means we will one day have a reunion, and what a great day that will be, but we don't have to wait for that day to come, we can act as children of our Heavenly Father now. He will ask you if you are serious by sending tests and trials. If you pass these, he will give you more, for if you can be trusted with a little, he will entrust you with more!

Soon, you will encounter opportunities to be His ambassador to the world, baring His likeness through deeds of compassion, joy and freedom, for orphans, widows, the impoverished, the oppressed, and those who are enemies of wrong-doers. He promises to reward our good deeds, when He returns in glory!

A. Destroyer of Evil

Read Romans 8: 37 – 39

Read 2 Corinthians 10: 3 – 6

Read Ephesians 5: 8 – 14

MICAH 7: 9

I will bear the indignation of the Lord, Because I have sinned against Him, Until He pleads my case and executes justice for me. He will bring me forth to the light; I will see His righteousness.

Prayer

Father, may we see our place is with you, as heirs, children. As David said, what are we that you have made us just under the angels but gave us this whole earth. Yet, we command the angels! People are dying for lack of hope and ministry, and the lack of angels to minister to the peoples of the earth. May we like the sower of seed, sow love and good news, and stay away from evil. Give us the spiritual weapons that have real power in our world and in the heavenly realms. Let us be on fire, bringing light, love, and consuming evil, in Jesus' name, Amen.

FOR DEEPER STUDY:

Micah 7 • Romans 8 • 2 Corinthians 10 • Ephesians 5

B. Judging the Angels

Read Isaiah 14: 9 – 10

Read Matthew 8: 28 – 31

Read 1 Corinthians 6:1 – 4

> MARK 16: 17
>
> *These signs will follow those who believe: in my name they will cast out demons; they will speak in tongues.*

Prayer

We see very little mentioned of these beings, except that they have chosen sides. Give us wise discerning hearts that allow us to entertain the good ones and defeat the lies, deception, and belief systems built by evil ones. Satan and his evil ones know that their time is coming and they are stirring up trouble daily, but in Christ, we have authority to command these to leave people, situations. Let us embrace you in truth, and ask you to work powerfully through us to judge evil doing, and allow your ministering angels to do their work, leading your people to their inheritance. Amen.

FOR DEEPER STUDY:

Genesis 1 • Job 1, 2 • 1 Kings 22 • Isaiah 14 • Zechariah 3 • Matthew 8 • Mark 16 • 1 Corinthians 6

C. Heirs & Coheirs

Read Acts 3: 24 – 26

Read Titus 3: 5 – 8

Read 1 Peter 3: 8 – 10

ROMANS 8: 17

...and if children, then heirs—heirs of God and joint heirs with Christ, if indeed we suffer with Him, that we may also be glorified together.

Prayer

Father, being benefactor of the earth, and heaven, and a sibling of Christ seems impossible, but I'm eternally grateful. Thank you for your promises to Abraham, your prophesies through the ages, your laws through Moses and your blessings to us in Christ Jesus. Your love is so amazing, so overwhelming, may our response be equally overwhelming to bystanders and those impacted by hurt, hatred, oppression, and sin. May grace abound in every one of us, as we continue to follow you. Make our love and motives and life story, from this day onward, be impossible for people to misinterpret. This we ask in Jesus' name, Amen.

FOR DEEPER STUDY:

Genesis 17 • Acts 3 • Titus 3 • 1 Peter 3 • Romans 8

D. Saints in Christ

Read 1 Corinthians 1: 1 – 3

Read 1 Thessalonians 3:11 – 13

Read Revelation 5: 7 – 9

> ROMANS 8: 28
>
> *And we know that all things work together for good to those who love God, to those who are the called according to His purpose.*

Prayer

Saints across the ages prayed to you, and showed love to their fellow man in other cities and countries as evidenced by Paul in his letters. May we continue this, not just for tradition's sake, but because you've called us to this, and it shows your love to a fractured, confused and lost people. May your love abound in us so that all who come to us find solace, refreshment, and life. Make me a channel of your peace, where there is hatred let me bring your love, where there is injury, your pardon Lord, and where there is doubt, true faith in you. (Prayer of St. Francis of Assisi) 13th Century.

FOR DEEPER STUDY:

Romans 8 • 1 Corinthians 1 • 1 Thessalonians 3 • Revelation 5

E. Instructing All (Including Children)

Read Psalm 78: 5 – 8

Read Romans 12: 6 – 8

Read 1 Timothy 4: 12 – 14

2 TIMOTHY 3: 16

All Scripture is given by inspiration of God, and is profitable for doctrine, for reproof, for correction, for instruction in righteousness.

Prayer

Lord you've promised that you will give us the gifts and means to make it happen for good because we are doing your will. Give us also strength and discernment as parents to teach our children your word, so that they may not sin against you. May we do all you want us to do without arguing or complaining, instead having gratitude in our hearts that you have called us to this work. Let us not overlook the young men and women who are on fire for you, but let us include them in service, to each other for you, so that the body may be built up. Amen.

FOR DEEPER STUDY:

Psalm 78 • Romans 12 • 1 Timothy 4 • 2 Timothy 3

F. Bride of Christ

Read Isaiah 54: 5 – 7

Read Matthew 6: 23 – 25

Read Revelation 21: 1 – 3

> MATTHEW 22: 37
>
> *Jesus said to him, "You shall love the Lord your God with all your heart, with all your soul, and with all your mind."*

Prayer

Satan tries to make us, who are made in your image, hate ourselves, using everything in this world, and even each other. Fill our eyes with your presence, with your plans for us and all those around us, let us be filled to overflowing, so others will see this too! Just as A bride and groom love each other, so let us hold firm to the faith that God will keep us, and deliver us, as he did the Israelites from Egypt. Adorn us with your loving kindness, and blessings, and help us to see you as a bride sees the bridegroom she loves. In Jesus name, Amen.

FOR DEEPER STUDY:

Isaiah 54 • Matthew 6, 22 • Revelation 21

G. Tried, Tested, & True

Read Psalm 17: 1 – 4

Read Isaiah 48: 9 – 11

Read Romans 12: 11 – 13

> 2 CORINTHIANS 11: 1 – 3
>
> *For I am jealous for you with godly jealousy. For I have betrothed you to one husband, that I may present you as a chaste virgin to Christ.*

Prayer

Father, may our prayers be filled with thanksgiving, exhortation, petition, and supplication to you. Making decisions is not enough, angels are saying, how serious are you? We will test your mettle. Hundreds of people from your family members to the people at work, to the post office, grocery store, and bank are watching you closely, so make sure your feet are planted surely on God and His word. May we follow the examples of the apostles, and saints around us, with you leading and guiding us. In Jesus' name, Amen.

FOR DEEPER STUDY:

Psalm 17 • Isaiah 48 • Romans 12

H. Vindicated by Christ

Read Psalm 17: 14 – 15

Read Colossians 1: 11 – 14

Read 1 Timothy 3: 15 – 16

> 1 JOHN 2: 11
>
> *But he who hates his brother is in darkness and walks in darkness, and does not know where he is going, because the darkness has blinded his eyes.*

Prayer

Father, may we continue to fix our gaze heavenward as the disciples did when Jesus ascended. You show yourself faithful, strengthening us, and showing all that you are the true way to freedom and joy. Remove our sins to present us to yourself blameless and pure, test us and see that we are committed to you and your ways. Let no temptation come our way but that which you will bring us through and help us to clearly see the path you have marked out for us. We have been set free. Help us to keep the Greatest Commandment to love you and our neighbor. Grant that your Spirit will confirm in us that we are yours, in Jesus' name, Amen.

FOR DEEPER STUDY:

Psalm 17 • Colossians 1 • 1 Timothy 3 • 1 John 2

I. Rewarded for Obedience

Read Deuteronomy 10: 12 – 14

Read 2 Corinthians 10: 5 – 7

Read Hebrews 11: 5 – 7

ROMANS 6: 16

Do you not know that to whom you present yourselves as slaves to obey, you are that one's slaves whom you obey, whether of sin, leading to death, or of obedience leading to righteousness?

Prayer

Father, we are sorry that our words, thoughts or actions may have been in service to the evil one, and we insist that we will ask you daily to lead us to do right, reshaping us in your image, and ways, making us obedient, and perfect, not only for yourself, but also as an example to others. May we be a shining example to others that obedience to your word brings rewards in this life and the life to come. Gift us with the tools to destroy strongholds, vanquish wrong beliefs and rumors. May there be no grey area in all matters. Give us faith to accomplish all that you give us to do so we cannot question it, in Jesus' name, Amen.

FOR DEEPER STUDY:

Deuteronomy 10 • Romans 6 • 2 Corinthians 10 • Hebrews 11

J. Bearers of Light

Read Acts 13: 46 – 48

Read 2 Corinthians 4: 5 – 7

Read 1 John 1: 6 – 8

2 THESSALONIANS 1: 10

When He comes, in that day, to be glorified in His saints and to be admired among all those who believe, because our testimony among you was believed.

Prayer

Father, thank you for Jesus, who light a light several thousand years. May we continue to shine brightly and go out courageously into this world with the intention each and every day to shine brightly so all may see what you are doing in and through our lives. Paul and Barnabas were faithful and truthful to speak the truth and encourage people that Jesus was the true way to right living. Continue to shine a light on our path and give us success, we pray, as you lead us forwards, until our world sees nothing but your light, in Jesus's name, Amen.

FOR DEEPER STUDY:

Acts 13 • 2 Corinthians 4 • 2 Thessalonians 1 • 1 John 1

CHAPTER 7

FATHER

(One God of all)

Exodus 20 • Ruth 2 • Isaiah 64

Any worship of anything besides God is idolatry, and is sin! God told the Israelites in the wilderness he was jealous of sin, but loved His children, and would love them for a thousand generations if they obeyed what He commanded. Our God extends this promise to us, His children, He is still jealous of sin, and He loves us.

After completing my education, I felt a little like Kevin Costner's character in *Dances with Wolves* when he requested a posting in the still uncharted western states. He would befriend the Sioux Warriors in the Dakotas. For the first little while I exalted in the different exercises and diversity in language, but I was not easily accepted.

Many remember the story of Abraham being told to count the grains of sand, or the stars in the sky. The story of Joseph was so well loved it has been made into a musical that includes his multi colored coat. But we sometimes forget that Rahab, the prostitute, and Ruth the Moabite were included in the genealogy of Jesus!

EXODUS 20: 14- 6

"You shall not make for yourself an image in the form of anything in heaven above or on the earth beneath or in the waters below. 5 You shall not bow down to them or worship them; for I, the Lord your God, am a jealous God, punishing the children for the sin of the parents to the third and fourth generation of those who hate me, 6 but showing love to a thousand generations of those who love me and keep my commandments.

A. I Am (Who I Am)

Read Exodus 3: 13 – 15

Read Leviticus 11: 44, 46

Read John 8: 46 – 50

> LEVITICUS 26: 1
>
> *You shall not make idols for yourselves; neither a carved image nor a sacred pillar shall you rear up for yourselves; nor shall you set up an engraved stone in your land, to bow down to it; for I am the Lord your God*

Prayer

From the beginning of time until now, you have made your mark on this world and its people. But you have also made it known who you are and whose you are, history shows the might of Israel, right up to and including the three-day war with Egypt in the 1970's. You alone are God. You commanded us to have none other than you, and we have been disobedient in this regard. God will reward every man for his (or her) works, so help us to do right in everything, thanking you for showing us we pray. Amen.

FOR DEEPER STUDY:

Exodus 3 • Leviticus 11, 26 • John 8

B. There Are Three That Testify

Read John 3: 13 – 17

Read John 8: 25 – 29

Read 1 John 5: 3 – 8

> 1 JOHN 4: 15
>
> *Whoever confesses that Jesus is the Son of God, God abides in him, and he in God.*

Prayer

Abide with me, fast flows the even tide, The darkness deepens Lord, with me abide. When other helpers fail and comforts flee Help of the helpless, oh, abide with me. (Henry Francias Lyte 1847 – LyricFind) Among many promises, Lord, is one that you abide with us, this more than any, is hope for each and every believer in Christ Jesus! May we share the news that you have saved the world, we need only believe and follow. In a world we find burdensome, let us offload every burden every curse, and every deception at the foot of the cross, and take on your commands. Give us assurance that we shall overcome. In Jesus's name, Amen.

FOR DEEPER STUDY:

John 3, 8 • 1 John 4, 5

C. Alpha

Read Genesis 1: 1 – 5

Read Exodus 13: 1 – 3

Read Exodus 20: 1 – 7

PSALM 139: 16

Your eyes saw my substance, being yet unformed. And in Your book, they all were written, the days fashioned for me, when as yet there were none of them.

Prayer

There is no power like yours, O Lord! There is no loving care like yours, no one is so meticulous, so loving, so compassionate, and so all-seeing. Though chaos ensued when Satan was cast to the earth, we thank you that you are on our side. Though we have day and night, there is nothing hidden from you. May we give our first, our best, our all. This is your greatest and first commandment. Most days we don't have anything, but we can count on you to give us what we need. May we be part of those thousand generations that you love, now and forevermore. For Jesus' sake, Amen.

FOR DEEPER STUDY:

Genesis 1 • Exodus 13, 20 • Psalm 139

D. Omega

Read Revelation 1: 7 – 9

Read Revelation 21: 5 – 7

Read Revelation 22: 12 – 14

REVELATION 22: 12

And behold, I am coming quickly, and My reward is with Me, to give to everyone according to his work.

Prayer

Father, yours is the last word, and we are thankful, for you are all, and in all things! Our grief and loss, our mourning over heartache, hurt, and anxiety are overwhelming, so offer us your words to satisfy our souls. The evil of this world will be judged and weighed carefully by Jesus in the great throne room that will one day dwarf heaven and earth. The heaven and earth will pass away, but His righteous judgments are forever, amen Lord so shall it be! May we ask daily to wash our robes and claim the blood of Jesus, that we might be found innocent at your coming, and find strength to do all that you call us to do. Amen.

FOR DEEPER STUDY:

Revelation 1 – 22

E. El Roi (All Seeing)

Read Psalm 2: 1 – 4

Read Psalm 33: 12 – 14

Read Psalm 139: 14 – 16

> 2 CORINTHIANS 4: 18
>
> *While we do not look at the things which are seen, but at the things which are not seen. For the things which are seen are temporary, but the things which are not seen are eternal.*

Prayer

Father, let us see beyond the lies, propaganda, and smoke and mirrors of experts, professionals, politicians, and leaders. Instead, fix our eyes on you, our maker, provider, refuge, and deliverer. You alone see all things and has planned from start to finish. Such knowledge is both exciting and mind-blowing! Even more so the changes of us into you, even though we feel squeezed, troubled, and sorrowful, help us to see that this is temporary, even necessary, to die, and you need to be born in us! Help us to abandon self, and become what we are meant to be. Amen.

FOR DEEPER STUDY:

Psalm 2, 33 • John 13 – 16 • 2 Corinthians 4 • 1 John 2

F. Judge of Nations

Read Psalm 110: 4 – 6

Read Joel 3: 11 – 13

Read Revelation 14: 18 – 20

REVELATION 8: 5

Then the angel took the censer, filled it with fire from the altar, and threw it to the earth. And there were noises, thunderings, lightnings, and an earthquake.

Prayer

Lord when our vision is not clear, or we do not understand things, it is easy for us to let our emotions to make us the judge and jury of poor decisions, actions, words and we forget who's in control here. All through the Old Testament we read of your judgments towards Egypt, the Nations of Caanan and their atrocities, the Philistines, and Assyrians, as noted in all the writings of the prophets, We await the judgment of Babylon and all within her. You are a just Judge, thank you, Amen.

FOR DEEPER STUDY:

Psalm 110 • Joel 3 • Revelation 8, 14

G. Abba Father

Read Deuteronomy 29: 27 – 29

Read Romans 8: 15 – 19 (We are family)

Read Revelation 7: 9 – 11

GALATIANS 4: 7

Therefore you are no longer a slave but a son, and if a son, then an heir of God through Christ.

Prayer

Father, thank you for making a place for us like you made a place for Israel, driving out the nations of evil that resided in Canaan. You revealed your strength and intentions by giving us the Ten Commandments, and you sent your Son, Jesus into this world to reveal our true nature as the beings you love in your creation! How magnificent that we should be called children of the God of earth and heaven, and we shall witness the destruction of these and the forces of wickedness, and be with you forever! I feel unworthy, but instead, let me and all who follow you, respond with gratitude in our hearts and thanksgiving, in Jesus' name, Amen.

FOR DEEPER STUDY:

Deuteronomy 29 • Romans 8 • Galatians 4 • Revelation 7

H. Creator

Read Genesis 1: 27 - 30

Read Genesis 8: 20 - 22

Read Psalm 8: 3 - 5

PSALM 139: 14

I will praise You, for I am fearfully and wonderfully made; Marvelous are Your works, and that my soul knows very well.

Prayer

Lord, you made us in your image, and gave us the job of naming and caring for the animals. You gave Noah and his family the job of building an ark on land and getting the animals of the earth into it. You renewed your commitment to mankind to keep the seasons and not bring another catastrophic flood while the earth remains. You communicate with us and the angels and ask our opinion about things. We echo king David, who wondered aloud what is man that you are mindful of or care about us? I'd not even know that you considered us, "to die for." We look forward being reunited with the family. Amen.

FOR DEEPER STUDY:

Genesis 1, 8 • Psalm 8, 139

I. Provider

Read Psalm 32: 3 – 5

Read Zechariah 3: 4 – 6

Read John 17: 6 – 8

JAMES 1: 17

Every good gift and every perfect gift is from above, and comes down from the Father of lights, with whom there is no variation or shadow of turning.

Prayer

Thank you for providing for us all through history, and for bringing about your plans and timing. May we lose our stress and anxiety wondering how things are going to work and hold onto you in faith. Give us joy in your presence, let every illness disappear at your word, and let us feel like kings on the earth. Just as Jesus prayed for his Disciples, so we pray to you for ourselves and our friends and families that we will hang on your every word, and be pleased to do your will, fully satisfied and filled to overflowing with love, grace and compassion, giving thanks for all your gifts. Amen.

FOR DEEPER STUDY:

Psalm 32, 33 • Zechariah 3 • John 17 • James 1

J. Honored

Read Daniel 4: 33 – 35

Read Malachi 3: 16 – 18

Read 1 Corinthians 12: 24 – 27

JOHN 12: 26

If anyone serves Me, let him follow Me; and where I am, there My servant will be also. If anyone serves Me, him My Father will honor.

Prayer

Lord, I smile when judges are referred to as "your honor." It is a man who has given them that title, and others that address them as such, but we need to ask, do we honor you in all we do, say, and think? Are you honored by our work, play, and rest. Or eating and drinking or the way we conduct our affairs? Nebuchadnezzar did was humiliated until he understood where life comes from and who is in control. You name a distinction between those who serve you and those who will not. You organize events, meetings of people, words and circumstances, so we are built up together. You promise us much for our service of you, let us enjoy you and the blessings of life. Amen.

FOR DEEPER STUDY:

Daniel 1 – 12 • Malachi 3 • 1 Corinthians 12 • John 12

CHAPTER 8

EQUIPPED

(Infinite Grace)

Psalm 23 • 1 Thessalonians 4 • 2 Timothy 3

Do we see our works as praising him, or reproducing his creative powers? I think of some of the amazing engineering feats of the last century that have built 100 plus storey skyscrapers, battery operated cars and trucks, or put us on the moon. Do we make amazing things to praise Him that others can use each day?

God is our Father and the Lord is our shepherd, giving us peace and provisions, delivering us from harm, renewing our soul, and comforting us. We look to Him and others see that we have been with Him, just as the Israelites saw Moses when he had been with you. Bless your saints who do your will, let us put all our trust in you!

2 TIMOTHY 3: 14 - 17

But as for you, continue in what you have learned and have become convinced of, because you know those from whom you learned it, and how from infancy you have known the Holy Scriptures, which are able to make you wise for salvation through faith in Christ Jesus. All Scripture is God-breathed and is useful for teaching, rebuking, correcting, and training in righteousness, so that the servant of God may be thoroughly equipped for every good work.

Consider that all the things that befall you, whether good or bad, are shaping you and moving you where the Lord wants you to go and be. And His Spirit goes with you, helping your formation, into something incredible! By yielding to His will and doing it, we become like Him, and our character change give us hope that He will do all He has said in His word!

A. Hope

Read Esther 9: 1 – 3

Read Psalm 25: 1 – 5

Read Romans 5: 1 – 6

HEBREWS 6: 19

This hope we have as an anchor of the soul, both sure and steadfast, and which enters the Presence behind the veil.

Prayer

Like you, hope often appears at the eleventh hour, giving us an opportunity to breathe again! May our hope be firmly rooted in you, creator, provider, planner, the God who sees all. You care about each and every life you have created, and you can make a way when it seems there is no way. At the death of Jesus, the curtain of the temple to the Holy of Holies was torn in two from top to bottom; the prophesy came true that said God's place will now be with men. We can come unhindered to the throne room and meet with you, and your Spirit sent to us convicts us of sin se that we continue in your ways. I hope to see you and all my friends and family soon, including Jesus. Amen.

FOR DEEPER STUDY:

Esther 9 • Psalm 25 • Romans 5 • Hebrews 6

B. Belief

Read Job 11: 3 – 7

Read John 12: 35 – 38

Read 2 Thessalonians 2: 13 – 17

> 1 TIMOTHY 4: 10
>
> *For to this end we both labor and suffer reproach, because we trust in the living God, who is the Savior of all men, especially of those who believe.*

Prayer

Thank you, Father for giving us the stories of people like Job, or king David, or Gideon. None were perfect, but they believed, and that was enough for you to use them! We pray that you would give us more faith that our belief would increase and doubt would disappear. It is okay that we do not understand all the mysteries of life, that we do not know everything about you, only that you have a plan for each and everyone of us and are ready to make it happen; make us children of light, until the darkness in our world vanishes, and your message goes to all you have prepared to hear it. Keep encouraging and strengthening us in Jesus' name, Amen.

FOR DEEPER STUDY:

Job 11 • John 12 • 1 Timothy 4 • 2 Thessalonians 2

C. Assurance

Read 1 Timothy 3: 13 – 17

Read Hebrews 10: 19 – 23

Read Hebrews 11:1 – 4

> ISAIAH 32: 17
>
> *The work of righteousness will be peace, And the effect of righteousness, quietness and assurance forever.*

Prayer

Thank you, Father that we do not need to ask for assurances, we have you, we have the example of Jesus, and the guarantee of the Holy Spirit, we also see the work of the fellow saints in the world today. May this good news eclipse any negative news story on the airwaves, or livestream. Further to this, we have assurance of forgiveness of sins. Jesus is forever to be praised and thanked for the blood sacrifice that takes away sin, and the baptism that gives us your Spirit. Abraham did not receive what was promised but believed that what you assured him of would come to pass. May we be this righteous, and committed, bringing peace to our souls and those of the people who surround us in life, from this day onward and forever. Amen.

FOR DEEPER STUDY:

Isaiah 32 • 1 Timothy 3 • Hebrews 10, 11

D. Confidence

Read 2 Chronicles 32: 7 – 10

Read Jeremiah 17: 6 – 8

Read Hebrews 13: 5 – 7

> 1 JOHN 5: 14
>
> *Now, this is the confidence that we have in Him, that if we ask anything according to His will, He hears us.*

Prayer

You will not allow us to see ruin, so long as our minds are focused on doing your will. Many point to the conquests and deaths recorded in God's word, but this little is mentioned of the atrocities committed by these nations and peoples. May our trust in you continue to grow as we live day by day in your presence, fearing nothing and looking to you to supply our needs. Jesus said, do not fear the one who can destroy the body, but feat him who can take both body and soul and cast them into hell. Hear this and every prayer we make in Jesus' name. Amen.

FOR DEEPER STUDY:

2 Chronicles 32 • Jeremiah 17 • Hebrews 13 • 1 John 5

E. Provide

Read Genesis 22: 13 – 17

Read Psalm 111: 7 – 10

Read Hebrews 1: 1 – 4

PHILIPPIANS 4: 19

And my God shall supply all your need according to His riches in glory by Christ Jesus.

Prayer

Father, many of us read the account of Abraham and Isaac on Mount Moriah, and we cringe, doubting we could act in faith as Abraham did, or believe on you to deliver us from such an act. But as we have read, you blessed him and we are witness because we are his descendants. May we fear nothing on this earth, or in life, but you, and may we shy away from doing everything but your will. Let us shine with truth and fairness as we do your will in the lives of others and in our workplaces. Thank you, for your generous supply for everyone who believes on you. Amen.

FOR DEEPER STUDY:

Genesis 22 • Psalm 111 • Philippians 4 • Hebrews 1

F. Distribute

Read Isaiah 34: 16 – 17

Read Mark 8: 6 – 8

Read 1 Corinthians 12: 7 – 11

EPHESIANS 4: 8

Therefore, He says: "When He ascended on high, He led captivity captive, and gave gifts to men."

Prayer

Father, you make the rain fall on the righteous and unrighteous, we have day and night and seasons that follow each other. You asked Job where the stores of snow are, and like us, he could not answer. In times of drought, you gave what was needed to your prophets. You blessed the gift of a boy who gave seven loaves and a few small fishes, feeding four thousand men. Praises be to your Spirit, who gives to each believer according to the gift apportioned to them that the body of Christ's bride, the church should be built up. Jesus promised when he ascended that he would give to us the Holy Spirit, so that God's dwelling will be with men. There will always be enough distributed to those of us who believe that we have everything God supplies. Amen.

FOR DEEPER STUDY:

Isaiah 34 • Mark 8 • 1 Corinthians 12 • Ephesians 4

G. Promise

Read Acts 1: 3 – 5

Read Acts 13: 31 – 33

Read Hebrews 12: 25 – 27

ACTS 2: 17

And it shall come to pass in the last days, says God, That I will pour out of My Spirit on all flesh; Your sons and your daughters shall prophesy, your young men shall see visions, your old men shall dream dreams.

Prayer

Thank you for the gift of your promised Holy Spirit. We don't often see eye to eye, but it makes us aware of sin and when we are in tune with each other we feel really good inside. It intercedes for us and helps us discern things that are right and wrong. Thank you for this immeasurable gift. As promised in your word, you will shake the earth, when this happens, may your Spirit strengthen us and help us to stand while thousands around us fall. Harm and pestilence will hit unbelievers, but you've promised to never leave or forsake us. Amen.

FOR DEEPER STUDY:

Acts 1, 2, 13 • Hebrews 12

H. Guarantee

Read Romans 4: 16 – 17

Read 2 Corinthians 5: 4 – 7

Read Ephesians 1: 7 – 15

> 2 CORINTHIANS 6: 16
>
> *And what agreement has the temple of God with idols? For you are the temple of the living God. As God has said: "I will dwell in them and walk among them. I will be their God, and they shall be My people."*

Prayer

Lord, thank you for opening our eyes to the idea of contracts that are legally binding! You made a contract with Abraham, and extended it to all who call him Father. You would clarify this to the people of Israel while in the wilderness of Caanan, and required sacrifice for sins, and a commitment to follow you with our heart, mind and soul! You yourself sent us your Spirit so that we would be covered in the blood of Jesus and counted as one of yours. Help us to see how you have lavished on us grace and mercy, and are destined to be yours for an eternity! Only Jesus' blood can seal the deal, may we praise him and forever be grateful, giving him thanks. Amen.

FOR DEEPER STUDY:

Romans 4 • 2 Corinthians 5, 6 • Ephesians 1

I. Refinement

Read Psalm 66: 5 – 12

Read Daniel 12: 8 – 11

Read 1 Peter 1 : 3 – 9

PHILIPPIANS 2: 15

That you may become blameless and harmless, children of God without fault in the midst of a crooked and perverse generation, among whom you shine as lights in the world.

Prayer

Father, may one and all see what you have done in our lives, and the free gift that is their's that believe in you. Let your praises never stop, for we are being made new day by day by the trials of this life, you are making us more like yourself. May we, like Daniel not worry about the "When," but the "How." You do these things and call us to tell the world all that you have done. The life that is resurrected in Spirit gives us an inheritance that will never spoil, this is why Jesus said, set up treasures in heaven. Whatever trials we face now, even the destruction of heaven and earth with fire will not compare to the rewards that will be ours in Christ. Amen.

FOR DEEPER STUDY:

Psalm 66 • Daniel 12 • Matthew 6 • 1 Peter 1 • Philippians 2

J. Anointing

Read Psalm 28: 6 – 9

Read Luke 4: 16 – 19

Read 2 Corinthians 1: 20 – 22

> PSALM 4: 3
>
> *But know that the Lord has set apart for Himself him who is godly; The Lord will hear when I call to Him.*

Prayer

Father, in many ways we feel untouchable, like we can do no wrong. Though we will encounter trials and difficulties, your hand is with us, we cannot fail, this is amazing and scary too. Let our response be one of gratitude and wonder, asking what you will have us do next? This is what gives our Lord His due, and we are grateful to do it. Your Spirit gave Jesus the ability to complete his ministry and tasks on earth, including his death and resurrection from the dead. We know that the miracles He did, were also the work of the Spirit, because you were in agreement that they should be done. Give us strength to stand firm when people, principalities and kingdoms set themselves against you. Thank you that you hear our prayers Lord, in Jesus' name, amen.

FOR DEEPER STUDY:

Psalm 4, 28 • Luke 4 • 2 Corinthians 1

PART 3

ABIDE

(Eternal love)

John 15:3 – 6 • Romans 8: 30 – 32 • Hebrews 12: 6 – 8

ISAIAH 50: 10

Who among you fears the Lord and obeys the word of his servant? Let the one who walks in the dark, who has no light, trust in the name of the Lord and rely on their God.

Prayer

Father, we know that like the Israelites we are a wayward people, let not the lessons you give us be so hard that we fail to see you as gracious, loving and the one who first loved and chose us. Give us passion to hod on tight and never let go of you, whatever happens, we may finish this life saying this was a wild ride, but that is preferred to the horror of hearing, "I never knew you, depart from me." You made us and love us, and wish for us to act like your legitimate children, so show us the way, and show us love, safety and support when needed, and discipline us when necessary. Help us to see that in your arms, nothing can harm us, so shall we be a light in a dark world, helping others to see the way to you is through no one but Jesus. Amen.

FOR DEEPER STUDY:

Isaiah 50 • John 15 • Romans 8

CHAPTER 9

BEING

(Who/Whose You Are)

Numbers 33 • Psalm 16 • John 4

As children, my siblings and I were amused by the dialogue on television that suggested a low life was a "Dirt-bag!" But I can also remember someone saying to me, "Oh, for heaven's sake, behave."

God chose the people of Jacob, and used Moses to lead them out of Egypt, utterly annihilating their army. God instructed them to depose the peoples of Canaan, and destroy their idols and practices, so that nothing remained to tempt the people of Israel. Instead, they adopted these. God was offended and incensed.

God calls us today to live by the Spirit. Jesus confronted the leader of the Pharisees, Nicodemus. But Jesus told him, what you seek to do as a dirt bag is impossible, only by Spirit can one come to the kingdom of heaven.

PSALM 16: 8 - 11

I keep my eyes always on the Lord. With him at my right hand, I will not be shaken. Therefore my heart is glad and my tongue rejoices; my body also will rest secure, because you will not abandon me to the realm of the dead, nor will you let your faithful one see decay. You make known to me the path of life; you will fill me with joy in your presence, with eternal treasures at your right hand.

Jesus alone is worthy of our praise for all that he has done, and he calls us friends and brothers, we have been given this world, to live, to thrive, to lead, (as the head, not the tail) and minister to those who need to know God. He is our inheritance, and is worthy of all our worship, now and forever.

A. Demolisher of Evil

Read Numbers 33: 51 – 53

Read Lamentations 3: 19 – 23

Read 2 Corinthians 10: 4 – 6

ZECHARIAH 4: 6

So he answered and said to me: "This is the word of the Lord to Zerubbabel: 'Not by might nor by power, but by My Spirit,' says the Lord of hosts.

Prayer

Nothing compares to the power of your spirit, who can do much greater things, and even small things. You commanded the Israelites to destroy the idolatry and death that reigned in the hearts and minds of the nations that resided there before them, but these overpowered them and they themselves forsook their God for these. Jeremiah would recount that you are faithful despite our sin, and you give us a fresh start every day. May we rely on the Spirit and the Word of truth to win the war, and destroy strongholds, but we need to show up and fight. After this, we can rest from our labours. Thank you, Lord, amen.

FOR DEEPER STUDY:

Numbers 33 • Lamentations 3 • Zechariah 4 • 2 Corinthians 10 • Hebrews 4

B. Judge of Angels & Circumstances

Read Isaiah 32: 16 – 18

Read 1 Corinthians 6: 1 – 4

Read Revelation 20: 4 – 5

> 1 CORINTHIANS 4: 4
>
> *I do not even judge myself. For I know of nothing against myself, yet I am not justified by this; but He who judges me is the Lord.*

Prayer

Lord, we so easily claim the bench and gavel when we feel wronged by others. It is your Spirit that renders judgments, not our overactive emotions. Help us to understand surrender to you, to seek the truth of your word and your will, and seek a peaceful resolution wherever possible. We are called to bring all things to your presence, whether that is in the stillness of the morning, the hustle and bustle of our days, or while we lay still on our beds. You are our judge and Satan is on the way out, so help us to know rightly how to conduct our lives, now and eternally. Amen.

FOR DEEPER STUDY:

Isaiah 32 • 1 Corinthians 4, 6 • Revelation 20

C. Saints in Christ

Read Psalm 16: 1 – 4

Read Ephesians 4: 11 – 13

Read Revelation 11: 16 – 19

1 CORINTHIANS 1: 2

To the church of God which is in Corinth, to those who are sanctified in Christ Jesus, called to be saints, with all who in every place call on the name of Christ our Lord, both theirs and ours:

Prayer

Just as David prayed, so we call on you to preserve our lives to do your will in and through our lives! Show us how our diversity means unity in your Church and your world, reaching the lost and building one another up. May we seek to become a mirror image of you, and work to praise your name and lift you up, until all the earth sees you. May we thank you in advance for your rewards, for the workers of darkness, eternal judgment, for the saints of light, heavenly rewards that we cannot imagine. May the saints celebrate you and rejoice that our names are written in the Lambs book of life. In Jesus' name, Amen.

FOR DEEPER STUDY:

Psalm 16 • 1 Corinthians 1 • Ephesians 4 • Revelation 11

D. The Rescuers

Read Zechariah 3: 1 – 4

Read Ezekiel 22: 29 – 31

Read Matthew 5: 14 – 20

LUKE 4: 18

The Spirit of the Lord is upon Me, Because He has anointed Me to preach the gospel to the poor; He has sent Me to heal the broken hearted, to proclaim liberty to the captives and recovery of sight to the blind, to set at liberty those who are oppressed;

Prayer

Thank you, Lord, for giving us this rare glimpse from your word of the things that happen beneath the veil. When the lives of all in heaven and on earth hang in the balance, it is great that you are there to weigh our obedience to you, and rebuked the accuser and destroyer of lives. May we stand in the gap for you, showing ourselves strong in faith, but also compassionate and forgiving, showing a way for all who are oppressed, troubled in soul, and feeling hopeless. Let us be light and life, glorifying God in all we say and do, to the glory of Christ Jesus. Amen

FOR DEEPER STUDY:

Zechariah 3 • Ezekiel 22 • Matthew 5 • Luke 4

E. Eyes on the Prize

Read Ezekiel 10: 4 – 5

Read Psalm 119: 76 – 78

Read 2 Corinthians 13: 5 – 8

EPHESIANS 4: 4

There is one body and one Spirit, just as you were called in one hope of your calling; one Lord, one faith, one baptism;

Prayer

Lord, we ask for eyes and ears of Spirit, to know the vision of things to come, may we yearn for your love, grace and peace in our lives. Grant us eyes that show us the path you have made for us, and a mind that does not go to the right or left of this path, for you give us good things in every day of our lives. Comfort us when the way is difficult, and we lack the strength and determination, show us mercy because your law is light and life. Help us to check our hearts, minds and Spirits to make sure we are still moving with you. Let us complete everything exactly as you require, with you helping us, so that nobody is in doubt, and your people are unified in one voice to praise you. Amen.

FOR DEEPER STUDY:

Ezekiel 10 • Psalm 13 • 2 Corinthians 13 • Ephesians 4

F. Teachers of Love & Truth

Read Matthew 5: 18 – 20

Read John 13: 33 – 35

Read Hebrews 8: 10 – 12

JAMES 1: 25

But he who looks into the perfect law of liberty and continues in it, and is not a forgetful hearer but a doer of the work, this one will be blessed in what he does.

Prayer

Father, we feel underqualified to be teachers of your love and truth. We know that your word is gospel, and law. Thank you for also giving us your Son as an example, and your Spirit to influence our actions and words. May we one day visit orphans (and the aged) in their trouble, heal the sick and help the poor. Many of us find it difficult to love our families when they are disagreeable, or rebellious, help us to continue to love one another. We long for the day when every living being knows your name, O Lord. From now on, let us live in the hope that all who hear of you from now on will rejoice that they have a savior and Lord. And your forgiveness. This we ask in Jesus' name, amen.

FOR DEEPER STUDY:

Matthew 5 • John 13 • Hebrews 8 • James 1

G. Tried, Tested, & True

Read Psalm 17: 2 – 4

Read Psalm 66: 9 – 11

Read 1 Thessalonians 3: 1 – 4

> 1 PETER 5: 10
>
> *But may the God of all grace, who called us to His eternal glory by Christ Jesus, after you have suffered a while, perfect, establish, strengthen, and settle you.*

Prayer

How I wish, O Lord, someone had told me about these tests when I was young. I continue to struggle through them, but now I know that they are for my good, because you are changing me into the person you want me to be. Many times, in the past, I would have buckled under the trials and agonized that you would hurt me, but you preserved my soul. Though our bodies remain (some until you return) may our old self die off, replaced by the person you made us to be. Let your Spirit reassure us in these times that you will strengthen and place us in pleasant secure pastures, and give us a place for all who are called to hear your gospel message. These things we ask in Jesus' name, amen.

FOR DEEPER STUDY:

Psalm 17, 66 • 1 Thessalonians 3 • 1 Peter 5

H. Binding & Loosing

Read Numbers 30: 2 – 4

Read Psalm 61: 1 – 6

Read Matthew 18: 17 – 19

HEBREWS 9: 15

And for this reason He is the Mediator of the new covenant, by means of death, for the redemption of the transgressions under the first covenant, that those who are called may receive the promise of the eternal inheritance.

Prayer

Thank you, Father, for appointing a mediator, Christ Jesus, who is able to judge the vows and binding contracts and spirit of mankind, and binds or loses these according to your will and ours! Just as a father's observance of a child's vow is observed and heard, so too do you hear ours. May we abide by you and the vows made, and may we bind ourselves forever to you so that nothing else will stick with us. Give us power, I pray to bind evil spirits and please destroy the work of the deceiver in the lives of those meant to come to you. Thank you for redeeming us from our transgressions and give is grace to forgive all who've wronged us. Amen.

FOR DEEPER STUDY:

Numbers 30 • Psalm 61 • Matthew 18 • Hebrews 9

I. Gapping Dirt & Spirit

Read Psalm 51: 7 – 11

Read Isaiah 26: 8 – 10

Read Romans 8: 22 – 24

> 2 CORINTHIANS 5: 20
>
> *Now then, we are ambassadors for Christ, as though God were pleading through us: we implore you on Christ's behalf, be reconciled to God.*

Prayer

Father, its surprising to us who have the whole Word of God to read to see that you searched the earth for one who would stand in the gap. We know that the only one who could, was Christ Jesus, the perfect sacrifice. Rightly, we cry create in me a clean heart, may this by our request to you daily. In all our deeds and words may your enemies be forgotten and your name remembered. We long for the resurrection, but we also have hope for lost souls who are friends and relatives, and so we will continue to stand in the gap. It is a life and death struggle, and we do not understand the cost Jesus paid, but were glad its paid. Amen.

FOR DEEPER STUDY:

Psalm 51 • Isaiah 26 • Romans 8 • 2 Corinthians 5

J. Spiritually Eternal

Read Mark 3: 28 – 30

Read Luke 16: 22 – 25

Read Revelation 14: 9 – 11

1 JOHN 5: 20

And we know that theSon of God has come andhas given us an understanding, that we may know Him who is true; and we are in Him who is true, in His Son Jesus Christ. This is the true Godand eternal life.

Prayer

Thank you, father, for sharing your creation, and your love with us. Jesus' death and sacrifice were an amazing thing and show your commitment to yo9ur creations. I can only imagine, indeed! May we not forget the story Jesus taught of Lazarus and the rich man. We know that in the story of the Israelites and in your laws, Idolatry is forbidden. May we now and forever see you as the object of our worship. May the thoughts, words, and deeds of our day to day lives find our names in the Lamb's book of life, and your mark on our head, so the beast can never put his mark there. Amen.

FOR DEEPER STUDY:

Mark 3 • Luke 16 • 1 John 5 • Revelation 14

CHAPTER 10

FOLLOW

(Choose to Serve Christ)

Joshua 24: 14 – 16 • Micah 6: 6 – 8 • 1 Thessalonians 1: 4 – 8

Everywhere on social media, we hear people who make video clips tell us to "follow me." But what does this mean exactly? Well, some want to influence you, others want to sell you things. Writer and pastor Andy Stanley suggests we follow Jesus, and he changes us when we do.

During the 40 years in the wilderness the Israelites endured that included the biblical books of Exodus, Leviticus, Numbers and Deuteronomy, we see that the people struggled with control. They had what they needed, but were discontent, they were lead but wanted to do their own thing. Even Moses got into it and as a result missed out on being able to enter the promised land. Joshua told them to choose one God and follow.

The prophet Micah, like many prophets and great rulers before him pondered what does God require of us? His response rings true with the Greatest Commandment. Indeed, Jesus himself had the greatest sales pitch when his ministry began, he invited his disciples, and they followed!

MATTHEW 4: 14 - 22

As Jesus was walking beside the Sea of Galilee, he saw two brothers, Simon called Peter and his brother Andrew. They were casting a net into the lake, for they were fishermen. "Come, follow me," Jesus said, "and I will send you out to fish for people." At once, they left their nets and followed him. Going on from there, he saw two other brothers, James, son of Zebedee and his brother John. They were in a boat with their father Zebedee, preparing their nets. Jesus called them, and immediately they left the boat and their father and followed him.

A. Blinded by Sin

Read John 12: 37 – 40

Read Romans 1: 21 – 23

Read 2 Corinthians 4: 1 – 5

JAMES 1: 25

But he who looks into the perfect law of liberty and continues in it, and is not a forgetful hearer but a doer of the work, this one will be blessed in what he does.

Prayer

Father, we now understand what a tangled web the deceiver has weaved during his time here on earth. Our world is confounded, tossed to and fro by the words of strong-willed men, and people who are themselves led astray by their blindness. We have the light of life, and I'm amazed that you should show us the way and allow others doubt and shame and sin to allow them to not want to find their way to you. We pray that you would strip the devil of his powers to blind people. We acknowledge that there is a choice on our part to be disobedient, but many are looking for a savior, and cannot see you for the darkness. Let's meet them in the middle and shine His light on them. Amen.

FOR DEEPER STUDY:

John 12 • Romans 1 • 2 Corinthians 4 • James 1

B. Joyful Faith Expressions

Read Deuteronomy 12: 5 – 7

Read Psalm 35: 4 – 10

Read Isaiah 25: 8 – 10

> 1 PETER 1: 8
>
> *Though now you do not see Him, yet believing, you rejoice with joy inexpressible and full of glory, receiving the end of your faith—the salvation of your souls.*

Prayer

Father, when we consider all that you have done for us, it is mind blowing, let this blossom into a heart that is overflowing with joy, giving praise to you and showing in everything we do that we are loved, prized, saved, and children of God! May we see and rejoice, over your victories in the lives of individuals and nations, just as you destroyed the Egyptian army when the Israelites went into the wilderness. May the peoples of the world see and put their trust in you, for this joy is contagious. Thank you for the death and resurrection of Jesus, and rejoice in the life to come.

FOR DEEPER STUDY:

Deuteronomy 12 • Psalm 35 • Isaiah 25 • 1 Peter 1

C. Invited by God

Read Isaiah 55: 1 – 3

Read Matthew 11: 27 – 29

Read Galatians 3: 26 – 29

MATTHEW 22: 12

So, he said to him, "Friend, how did you come in here without a wedding garment?" And he was speechless.

Prayer

Thank you for your invitation. Some think it too good to be true, may your word be an open book to us, revealing to us every truth and lead us in the path of righteousness. May all come to you to learn and be changed, for we do not see what we could be, but the one who made us knows all the mysteries of life. Give us an adverturesome attitude that takes hold of your promises with both hands and does not look back. Give thy restless soul peace in the knowledge that you have everything under control, we just need to hold on! Thank you for your invitation to Abraham. You had to know he would obey, but he also had to make a bold move of faith to go wherever you lead, and so we need to make ourselves ready for you. Amen.

FOR DEEPER STUDY:

Isaiah 55 • Matthew 11, 22 • Galatians 3

D. Repentant Confession

Read Psalm 51: 1 – 3

Read Mark 2: 15 – 17

Read Acts 11: 12 – 15

> NEHEMIAH 9: 3
>
> *And they stood up in their place and read from the Book of the Law of the Lord their God for one-fourth of the day; and for another fourth they confessed and worshiped the Lord their God.*

Prayer

Father, we confess our sins, and we renounce them, we are no longer willing to be slaves to sin and Satan. Help us day by day to trust in you when old habits and temptations distract us from serving you. Make us stronger than these, and help us to rise to the joy of soaking in your presence and being blessed to see and hear your words, and to know we are loved by you. Thank you for coming to heal, to cleanse, to forgive and forget. May we learn all of these, and affect our world for the better, showing the love that is ours in Christ Jesus. May your word shout to us louder than the deceitful and poisonous words of Satan and his demons. May your Spirit protect us, reminding us whose we are.

FOR DEEPER STUDY:

Nehemiah 9 • Psalm 51 • Mark 2 • Acts 11

E. Find His Face

Read 2 Chronicles 7: 13 – 15

Read Psalm 27: 7 – 9

Read Jeremiah 29: 12 – 14

> PSALM 53: 2
>
> *God looks down from heaven upon the children of men, to see if there are any who understand, who seek God.*

Prayer

Father, we would not hide from you, in the darkness, because even the darkness is as light to you. Help us see that there is light all about us, and you are seeking us just as much as we seek you. May your word let us know where you are, and may we never wish to be away from your light, because that is how things become obscured. May life and truth abound with joy and peace. We need your love to be shown through our lives so grant us the tools to make this happen and make us dig deeper into your word and hear you speaking to our hearts, leading and directing us. We long to hear you say, "well done, good and faithful servant."

FOR DEEPER STUDY:

2 Chronicles 7 • Psalm 27, 53 • Jeremiah 29 • Micah 3

F. Loving Eyes

Read Genesis 1: 26 – 28

Read Psalm 8: 3 – 6

Read 1 Corinthians 15: 51 – 53

1 JOHN 3: 24

Now, he who keeps His commandments abides in Him, and He in him. And by this we know that He abides in us, by the Spirit whom He has given us.

Prayer

God of love, we, like David, wonder aloud, what are we that you are mindful of us? Revelations and Daniel describe your eyes as fiery, pure, incorruptible; many write about Jesus eyes as he hung on the cross as being filled with love. All we know is that you saw something special when you made us, and you are still making us. May we too receive loving eyes that see past those who are hurtful, deceiving, and greedy, to the soul that is frightened, hurt, and confused. May people see in our eyes a life forever changed and life that nothing else in the world can give. This we ask in the name of Jesus, Amen.

FOR DEEPER STUDY:

Genesis 1 • Psalm 8 • 1 Corinthians 15 • 1 John 3

G. Soul Manna

Read Job 23: 11 – 13

Read Ezekiel 44: 4 – 6

Read Micah 6: 7 – 8

> MATTHEW 5: 6
>
> *Blessed are those who hunger and thirst for righteousness, for they shall be filled.*

Prayer

At these times, Lord, be closer to us, we pray, and help us to realize you are with us in our trials. We know that our sins have estranged us from you, and we beg your forgiveness. Fill use each day, from your Holy word, that we might never die of hunger or thirst, and lead us in the way of life eternal. We know that we can not give enough to take away our sins, nothing we do can ever be enough. Thankfully, you do not ask for all we have, instead, you ask us to commit our lives to you, to follow your will and ways. We stand by, arms raised high, willing and ready to be filled with your living water and spiritual manna, Amen.

FOR DEEPER STUDY:

Job 23 • Ezekiel 44 • Micah 6 • Matthew 4 • Hebrews 13

H. Bearing Fruit & Light

Read Galatians 5: 22 – 25

Read Philippians 2: 11 – 13

Read 1 John 4: 11 – 13

> PSALM 92: 14
>
> *Those who are planted in the house of the Lord shall flourish in the courts of our God. They shall still bear fruit in old age; They shall be fresh and flourishing.*

Prayer

Father, help us learn from Job, and share in his glory, having twice as much after his trials as before, not to gloat, but so that we can show how much you love us, and we will never doubt you. May our lives bear fruit, that shows love and respect for the law. May we live to excite everyone in the things that you have done, and that you would call us children! Help us to stand when the world pushes us down. May our love be evident to all who wonder what it is that makes us different, may the see love and give thanks to you. May every day of this life show you working in and through us to raise up your people, until the day you call us home. Amen.

FOR DEEPER STUDY:

Psalm 98 • Galatians 5 • Philippians 2 • 1 John 4

I. Wise, Thankful Ways

Read Ezra 3:9 – 11

Read 1 Thessalonians 5: 15 – 22

Read 1 Timothy 2: 1 – 4

PROVERBS 23: 15

My son, if your heart is wise, my heart will rejoice in the truth your lips speak.

Prayer

Isaiah said every one has gone his own way, but Jesus led us back to you. Let thanksgiving be a part of our every waking moment. Unlike those who become comfortable with traditions and dull routines, may we test ideas, theories, and belief systems, pushing aside every falsehood and embracing your truth. Just as refugees of the Ukrainian war pray for an end to it, let us join them in Spirit, and call all leaders to repentance. End wars, factions, oppression, and slavery, may no one be jealous of, or seek vengeance on another, that they all be subject to you. Amen.

FOR DEEPER STUDY:

Ezra 3 • Psalm 100 • Proverbs 23 • 1 Thessalonians 5 • 1 Timothy 2

J. Consuming Eyes of Purity

Read Daniel 10: 5 – 7

Read 1 Thessalonians 4: 1 – 3

Read Revelation 19: 11 – 13

JOHN 3: 14

And as Moses lifted up the serpent in the wilderness, even so must the Son of Man be lifted up.

Prayer

Forgive us, Lord, that our thoughts, words, and actions are not pure. And yet there cannot be love for one another or you if the purity does not come because there will always be a separation between us. I pray that the scales are removed and we see each other clearly, and others see love in our eyes, not our sins. Just as Paul called the Thessalonians to turn from sexual immorality, may many be saved of this generation who have fallen into this trap. Just as Moses lifted the snake in the wilderness, so let us raise you up that all may see and believe. Amen.

FOR DEEPER STUDY:

Daniel 10 • Psalm 73 • 1 Thessalonians 4 • Matthew 5 • John 3

CHAPTER 11

STAND

(Become Echos of Christ)

Romans 8: 17 - 19 • Colossians 2: 4 - 8 • Ephesians 6: 11 - 17

This world is filled with fear, shame, and pain on a scale that makes standing in the open as a follower of God seem like a lost cause. I got word yesterday that someone I cared about as a friend and a lover of life and family lost the battle with cancer. Today, I received an email that this disease is ravaging another! It is unsettling to think we gotta lay back and take it. I want to fight!

Proverbs 3 says, "Don't lean on your own understanding." Some call Christianity a crutch because of this, yet, it is the only rock on which to stand. No religious ideology or recantation can stop the armies of Satan, but he must obey the word of God, and so must we. In the Spirit, we show who we are. In the heat of the battle, it may seem we are losing, but we will rise up with Christ.

> ROMANS 8: 17 - 19
>
> *Now, if we are children, then we are heirs—heirs of God and co-heirs with Christ, if indeed we share in his sufferings in order that we may also share in his glory. I consider that our present sufferings are not worth comparing with the glory that will be revealed in us.For the creation waits in eager expectation for the children of God to be revealed.*

The image of David as a shepherd boy in soldiers armor makes me smile, but he was chosen of God and flung a stone into the skull of Goliath, killing the nemesis of the Israeli army for several months. The Philistines were silenced. So too, when tempted in the wilderness, Jesus silenced Satan by quoting God's word. When we take what God offers, and move forward in his Spirit, we can be confident to win.

A. He Is God of All

Read 2 Kings 19: 14 – 16

Read Psalm 57: 4 – 10

Read Ephesians 4: 3 – 7

EZRA 8: 22

For I was ashamed to request the king an escort of soldiers and horsemen to help us against the enemy on the road, because we had spoken to the king, saying, "the hand of our God is upon all those for good who seek Him, but His power and His wrath are against those that forsake Him.

Prayer

We thank you that there is no other. Though the curse on the earth, mankind and Satan means the waters are muddied, you continue to show yourself true, undefiled, and in control. May this continue, throughout this life and the life to come! Battles continue to wage, physically, mentally, and spiritually, when either becomes too much, let us take refuge under your wings, and show us your power, as your judgments and wrath are on display for all the world to see. Fill our hearts with gratitude and thanksgiving, knowing you have already won these battles. Amen.

FOR DEEPER STUDY:

2 Kings 19 • Ezra 8 • Psalm 57 • Ephesians 4

B. Incorruptible

Read 1 Peter 1: 3 – 5

Read 1 Peter 1: 22 – 24

Read 1 Peter 3: 3 – 6

> MATTHEW 6: 20
>
> *...but lay up for yourselves treasures in heaven, where neither moth nor rust destroys and where thieves do not break in and steal.*

Prayer

Thanks be to you, God, that you treasure us, the apple of your eyes, though Satan is jealous beyond reason, you have seen to his deceit, and his destruction is sure. Keep us safe from sin and destruction we pray, for in time, we will inherit our spiritual resurrection bodies, immaculate, incorruptible, beautiful! May we likewise treasure you, who lives in heaven, where you live, and from which we will receive the reward of our sanctified souls, and a life of joy and a life of serving you. That is an armor no game or organization could forge anywhere. It is truly amazing and formidable. Thank you for this priceless gift. Amen.

FOR DEEPER STUDY:

Matthew 6 • 1 Peter 1 – 3

C. Made in His Image

Read Genesis 1: 25 – 27

Read Genesis 9: 5 – 7

Read 1 Corinthians 11: 8 – 12

ISAIAH 44: 17

And the rest of it he makes into a god, His carved image. He falls down before it and worships it, Prays to it and says, "Deliver me, for you are my god!"

Prayer

Imitation is more than flattery, for you, o Lord made a proclamation when you made man in your image, you told the rest of the universe that you prized us above all else. As God, you call for us to prize you above all else, and not to make any images of anything, but to serve and obey you only. Your commitment to us is unswerving, and you have bound yourself to us, stating that you will lose us in heaven. I pray that they may see their folly and change before it is too late. Continue to show yourself to us more and more, so no image is necessary, one day we'll be face to face.

FOR DEEPER STUDY:

Genesis 1, 9 • Isaiah 44 • 1 Corinthians 11

D. Righteous

Read Psalm 111: 2 – 4

Read Psalm 112: 1 – 9

Read 2 Corinthians 9: 8 – 11

LUKE 6: 38

Give, and it will be given to you: good measure, pressed down, shaken together, and running over will be put into your bosom. For with the same measure that you use, it will be measured back to you.

Prayer

When I watch music videos showing exotic locations and vacation getaways, I am amazed by the beauty you have created. When I look at the woman who loves me, I am equally amazed! Sometimes, I'm one who feels I don't deserve it, other times I too easily take your loving kindness for granted. Please forgive me. Help me to, like you, give out of a heart of gratitude for all that you have given and done for me! Give to all who believe, your measure of love, faith, and blessing. Let us, together show your love to us and in turn, show love to so many more who have not. May our gratitude and thanksgiving abound.

FOR DEEPER STUDY:

Psalm 11, 112 • Luke 6 • 2 Corinthians 9

E. Purposed to Do Great Things

Read Isaiah 14: 23 – 28

Read Jeremiah 29: 10 – 12

Read Romans 8: 18 – 25

EPHESIANS 1: 11

In Him also we have obtained an inheritance, being predestined according to the purpose of Him who works all things according to the counsel of His will, 12 that we who first trusted in Christ should be to the praise of His glory.

Prayer

Amazingly, reading your word, I begin to wonder aloud, what purposes do you have for me in the life to come? Yes, that time will come, but for now, gird us with strength as in the days of Noah and king David to stand fast against unseen enemies. Many peoples stand in exile, awaiting a time or opportunity to return, like the prodigal son. Put peace in the hearts of those you wish to call forward, give wisdom and discernment to lead them forwards at the proper time. Persistence will be rewarded, for the Meek shall inherit the earth. Amen.

FOR DEEPER STUDY:

Isaiah 14 • Jeremiah 29 • Matthew 5 • Romans 8

F. Heirs

Read Romans 8: 14 – 18

Read Galatians 3: 26 – 32

Hebrews 6: 13 – 18

TITUS 3: 7

...that having been justified by His grace we should become heirs according to the hope of eternal life.

Prayer

I do not consider myself a brother of Jesus, but that is what you have done for us. When this world seems to dwarf us, may we reach out our hands and call to Daddy for help. All other things or beings to which we take hold are false hopes. We were baptized, into your death, your resurrection, your rebirth, and have received your Holy Spirit, who will guide us to the way of everlasting life. Your will and your word have made this possible, and we are unclear what it all means. Revel to us daily more of your plan and help us to faithfully move forwards into it, until we see nothing else.

FOR DEEPER STUDY:

Romans 8 • Galatians 3 • Hebrews 6 • Titus 3

G. Made Alive in the Spirit

Read Ephesians 2: 1 – 7

Read Colossians 2: 11 – 15

Read 1 Peter 3: 17 – 22

JOHN 5: 20

For the Father loves the Son, and shows Him all things that He Himself does; and He will show Him greater works than these, that you may marvel.

Prayer

Father, many of us live like we are dying, rather than like we are being made alive. Show us how it feels to be made alive in desiring to do your will, and removing the scales form the eyes of others who have little or no hope. Help us to forever bury our old habits, thought, ways of life, and beliefs. Eliminate fleshly thoughts, and fill our minds and hearts with Spiritual joys and ways that gladden your hearts and ours. We are letting your Spirit guide and direct, with you at the helm. Christ is the first fruit; we are heirs and we were meant to do greater things than he.

FOR DEEPER STUDY:

John 5 • Ephesians 2 • Colossians 2
• 1 Corinthians 15 • 1 Peter 3

H. Building, Budding, Blessed

Read Revelation 3: 11 – 13

Read John 15: 1 – 7

Read Matthew 25: 30 – 25

> 2 CORINTHIANS 12: 9
>
> *And He said to me, "My grace is sufficient for you, for My strength is made perfect in weakness." Therefore, most gladly I will rather boast in my infirmities, that the power of Christ may rest upon me.*

Prayer

Father, how amazing that you would not only see one to help build your church, but also make a pillar of those who overcome the enemy and write on us a new name. While we are not in control of how things play out, we are responsible, to make a decision to follow, which allows us to produce your fruit, seeing others come to faith in you. We choose to abide in you, and long to see you working through us. We long to hear, "well done, good and faithful servant." We know that we will have to suffer, for a little while, but even in this keep us strong and hopeful, that all will see you at work within our lives. Amen.

FOR DEEPER STUDY:

Matthew 25 • John 15 • 2 Corinthians 12 • Revelation 3

I. Freedom, Joy, & Service

Read Galatians 5: 1 – 6

Read Luke 15: 8 – 10

Read Jude 20 – 25

JAMES 1: 25

But he who looks into the perfect law of liberty and continues in it, and is not a forgetful hearer but a doer of the work, this one will be blessed in what he does.

Prayer

Thank you, Father for granting us freedom from sin, and giving us once again a choice, instead of sacrificing us for the sins of our ancestors, you have done what the law could not, and we are once again free to serve you in joy and grace. Likewise, we are surprised and joyful that you are so diligent to find one of who has gone missing. May we have peace in you and be motivated to serve with grateful hearts, filled with happiness for all you have done. May everything we think say and do be a pleasant aroma just as sacrifices of the past, with your word leading us forward. Amen.

FOR DEEPER STUDY:

Luke 15 • Galatians 5 • James 1 • Jude 20

J. Courage, Contend, Consider

Read Joshua 1: 6 – 8

Read Philippians 3: 10 – 15

Read Psalm 8: 1 – 4

2 TIMOTHY 3: 14

But you must continue in the things which you have learned and been assured of, knowing from whom you have learned them.

Prayer

May your every word, spoken through your moth and the mouth of Jesus, be so clear to us that nothing else can cloud our perception or our spirits. Make us intrepid towards the plans and schemes of the enemy, do not let us be distracted or led to the left or right, but only in the direction your Spirit leads. Let us, with arms open wide, long for your presence, and to be held, and carried over the highs and lows of life. Help use to not get stuck in this world's trappings, but free us to do right. May we glory in your steadfastness, and grace, showing the world by our conduct and conviction that we are truly yours. Amen.

FOR DEEPER STUDY:

Joshua 1 • Psalm 8 • Philippians 3 • 2 Timothy 3

CHAPTER 12

MULTIPLY

(Growing in Grace, and Faith)

Mark 4: 15 - 20 • John 14: 10 - 14 • Colossians 1: 9 - 14

I can remember early in my dating years, sharing in messages with a lady I met online, I referred to The Bible as Miracle Grow! It turns out not only did she like that, but she agreed, as many today seem to as well. With all the sights, games, vacations, adventures, entertainment and work that seems to abound, it still rings true that the more time I spend in God's word, the less I want to spend on other things.

John 3: 16 is the most quoted verse in modern days, but John 14: 12 is just as remarkable! Jesus tells us that Faith in Christ Jesus will allow us to receive favor with God the Father, so that we will be able to do more than we can imagine. In doing such things, we glorify the Father, and show the world that the Son, Jesus is alive in us, millions of believers who will do more than one man. The man in me gets excited just thinking about this... Let's go!

COLOSSIANS 1: 3 - 6

We always thank God, the Father of our Lord Jesus Christ, when we pray for you, because we have heard of your faith in Christ Jesus and of the love you have for all God's people—the faith and love that spring from the hope stored up for you in heaven and about which you have already heard in the true message of the gospel that has come to you. In the same way, the gospel is bearing fruit and growing throughout the whole world—just as it has been doing among you since the day you heard it and truly understood God's grace.

A. Filled With Light

Read Job 33: 28 – 30

Read Psalm 27: 1 – 5

Read Proverbs 6: 20 – 23

> 2 TIMOTHY 1: 7 - 11
>
> *... but has now been revealed by the appearing of our Savior Jesus Christ, who has abolished death and brought life and immortality to light through the gospel.*

Prayer

Fill us with the light of your spirit, giving light to our paths, illumination to your word, and knowledge to lead and guide us forwards. May the light of your redemption light the world in which we live and bring all things in conformity with you. May all who wish us harm stumble and fall, but we, oh Lord, stand firm on your promises. Let your word and your law be a constant in our lives, showing forth your light for others to follow your will and ways. When we think and speak, your Spirit will be our mouthpiece, so that we would not deceive. Amen.

FOR DEEPER STUDY:

Job 33 • Psalm 27 • Proverbs 6 • 2 Timothy 1

B. Banishing Darkness

Read Isaiah 9: 1 – 3

Read Isaiah 58: 6 – 11

Read 1 John 1: 1 – 6

ISAIAH 58: 10

If you extend your soul to the hungry and satisfy the afflicted soul, then your light shall dawn in the darkness, your darkness shall be as the noonday.

Prayer

Father, it is not enough to turn your back on darkness, because the darkness goes where there is no sunlight. May we multiply your light on all so they may see you at work and give you the glory. You used Isaiah to show the people of Israel what they must do to show forward your light to the world, even while they were in exile in Assyria. You showed us the importance of obedience and communication in moving your hand to move. Like us, you became a live and dwelt with us, showing yourself to be possible in human form, and leading us to follow and in doing so, have multiplied your light, and life and joy in the hearts of your people, banishing darkness in its wake, amen.

FOR DEEPER STUDY:

Isaiah 9, 58 • John 1 • 1 John 1

C. Bearing Spiritual Fruit

Read 1 Corinthians 14: 7 – 13

Read Galatians 5: 22 – 24

Read Ephesians 5: 8 – 12

JOHN 15: 5

"I am the vine; you are the branches. He who abides in Me, and I in him, bears much fruit; for without Me you can do nothing."

Prayer

Thank you, Father, for giving everything order, substance, and life. When we hear a symphony, where every singer and instrumentalist is directed by the conductor, and every note is crisp and distinct, we know that your ways and your plans are a result of this and we are glad. May each and every gift, deed, word, and effort be to your glory, so all mankind will be drawn to you. So too, may we, in showing love, exhibit the fruits of the Spirit, so that none may mistake whom we believe. May we continue, day after day to abide in you, so light will have the last word over darkness. Amen.

FOR DEEPER STUDY:

John 15 • 1 Corinthians 14 • Galatians 5 • Ephesians 5

D. Reject Wrong Pursuits

Read Colossians 2: 8 – 12

Read Galatians 1: 6 – 10

Read 2 John 1: 6 – 8

DEUTERONOMY 4: 23

Take heed to yourselves, lest you forget the covenant of the Lord your God which He made with you, and make for yourselves a carved image in the form of anything which the Lord your God has forbidden you.

Prayer

Father, let our minds, bodies, and souls be focused on what we need from you to accomplish your will, and ourselves and the people around us, that we may remain focused on doing what is right. May we remember your sacrifice on the cross, and the baptism with which you claimed us as righteous in your eyes. Keep your word fresh in our minds, and your Spirit sharp to show us when we err in our ways. In Jesus name we pray, Amen.

FOR DEEPER STUDY:

Deuteronomy 4 • Colossians 2 • Galatians 1 • 2 John 1

E. Purify Heart & Soul

Read Matthew 5: 27 - 30

Read John 12: 46 - 48

Read James 4: 3 - 9

TITUS 2: 14

...who gave Himself for us, that He might redeem us from every lawless deed and purify for Himself His own special people, zealous for good works.

Prayer

Father, thank you for giving us a display of your character, all through creation, your promises to Abraham, the Israelites you rescued from Egypt, and the life of Jesus. We know our little ones watch and hear all we do and say, but Jesus reminded us that the world likewise is watching us. He said that the words and actions of those who reject your words and laws judges them, not us. Help us to seek your will and ways, so that you will be pleased to grant us that which we stand in need of to accomplish them and live peaceably. Thank you for Jesus' work and the sacrament of baptism, to signify our cleansing. Amen.

FOR DEEPER STUDY:

Matthew 5, 6 • John 12 • Acts 19 • James 4 • Titus 2

F. Instruments of Righteousness

Read Romans 6: 16 – 18

Read Romans 8: 9 – 12

Read 2 Corinthians 4: 13 – 16

ROMANS 6: 13

And do not present your members as instruments of unrighteousness to sin, but present yourselves to God as being alive from the dead, and your members as instruments of righteousness to God.

Prayer

With so many seen and unseen beings operating within a system that is flawed, Lord, it is easy for us to become out of tune and in need of repair. We are called to love one another, but pressures abound, and we feel the squeeze. Help us to hold to your teachings and remember that we are yours. Grant that your Spirit gently reminds us in these times that we are yours and you are right here with us. We feel like death is winning, but you have the last word in any argument. Help us to flee the flesh, and seek your joy and refuge. Make grace a shield that covers us all and gives us strength to keep going, with your Spirit in us, lead us in your way. Amen.

FOR DEEPER STUDY:

Romans 6, 8 • 1 Corinthians 4

G. Forgiving Our Sins

Read Matthew 18: 31 – 35

Read Acts 10: 42 – 45

Read 2 Corinthians 2: 8 – 11

MARK 11: 25

And whenever you stand praying, if you have anything against anyone, forgive him, that your Father in heaven may also forgive you your trespasses.

Prayer

May grace the garland gracing our necks, ever present. We wish to overflow with mercy, knowing your grace is infinite. We know that you are the judge of all, so we have no excuse for laying a hand on another human being. Help us to forgive sins, showing ourselves to be your children, and in turn, drawing all to a compassionate, and forgiving God. Thank you that forgiveness is available to all people, just as the gospel, and your Spirit are available to all. If anything stands in the way of our forgiveness, or our relationship with other, remove it we pray. Amen.

FOR DEEPER STUDY:

Isaiah 33 • Matthew 18 • Mark 11 • Acts 10 • 2 Corinthians 2

H. Healing Other's Hurts

Read Isaiah 58: 7 – 9

Read Proverbs 12: 17 – 19

Read Acts 14: 9 – 11

LUKE 6: 42

Or how can you say to your brother, "Brother, let me remove the speck that is in your eye," when you yourself do not see the plank that is in your own eye? Hypocrite! First remove the plank from your own eye, and then you will see clearly to remove the speck that is in your brother's eye.

Prayer

Father, our responses should be patient, loving, and peaceful, not violent, angry or upset by the world's actions or the enemy's tactics. With the Spiritual weapons you employ, tear down strongholds of lies, deception, injustice, and oppression, and grant us a right Spirit to lead and guide. Help us instil goodness, decency, and grace in others, and a faith that wills healing, inner peace, and love. Let your Spirit be loosed into every situation that needs wisdom, grace, clarity, and healing, so may together give you all the glory and thanks you are due. Amen.

FOR DEEPER STUDY:

Isaiah 58 • Proverbs 12 • Luke 6 • Acts 14

I. Laying Our Lives on the Line

Read John 10: 13 – 15

Read John 15: 12 – 14

Read 1 John 3: 15 – 17

> 2 TIMOTHY 1: 10
>
> *... but has now been revealed by the appearing of our Savior Jesus Christ, who has abolished death and brought life and immortality to light through the gospel,*

Prayer

Father, we, like sheep, wander often from the fold, yet even now Psalm 23 rings in my ears, and I wait patiently for your voice to lead me where you need me to be. Help us to remain obedient to you and not act wrongly. You lead by example, and call us to love one another because it covers a lot of wrongs. Help me to be selfless, and obedient. Make us also as generous as you are so that the light of your love will shine that much brighter and bless more people in believing and changing for you have made us all in your image. Make new life visible through us, and give us peace in your arms. In Jesus name we pray, Amen.

FOR DEEPER STUDY:

John 10 • John 15 • 2 Timothy 1 • 1 John 3

J. Leading All to Eternity

Read Matthew 13: 5 – 11

Read John 4: 13 – 16

Read Galatians 6: 6 – 10

> HEBREWS 8: 11
>
> *None of them shall teach his neighbor, and none his brother, saying, 'Know the Lord,' for all shall know Me, from the least of them to the greatest of them.*

Prayer

Father, fill us every day with seed, and prompt us to take it everywhere, that we would sow love, joy, peace, and hope into the lives of all we come in contact with. Let us not become discouraged when the seed does not produce, instead, give us many opportunities to sow your goodness into the lives of all. Add to this also your living water, so that none should be parched, but let us soak in your presence, your love, your protection, and show us how to live a life of love. Give to each of us a measure of growth, help us, like the kernel of weight to crucify the old self and like Paul count our old gains as loss compared to you. In Jesus' name, amen.

FOR DEEPER STUDY:

Matthew 13 • John 4 • Galatians 6 • Hebrews 8

PART 4

WILLING

(Thy will be done)

Judges 5: 1 – 3 • Matthew 26:41 – 43
• 1 Corinthians 15: 57 – 59

ISAIAH 1: 19

If you are willing and obedient, you will eat the good things of the land;

Prayer

Father, does our inner being shake when we hear your voice? Grant us a heart that seeks your will and your Spirit's leading in every thought, word, and action, constantly praying for and giving care and compassion through our work, play, and service to our families, friends, and coworkers. May this attitude fill us with a heart of praise, and joy that our God reigns. It is man's will and way to control outcomes, and have the upper hand, but when we surrender our will to you, your will is done, and we reap a blessing and very great reward. "Trust and obey, for there's no other way, to be happy in Jesus!" [John H Sammis 1887]

FOR DEEPER STUDY:

Judges 5 • Isaiah 1 • Matthew 26 • 1 Corinthians 15

CHAPTER 13

LIKENESS

(Sanctified, remade)

Isaiah 14 • Ezekiel 2 • Luke 9 • 1 Peter 1

So many stand in their own strength, planning and scheming with friends in order to rise above, and be the one to free all from their bondage. Sound familiar? Who tried to convince Adam and Eve they would be "Like God," knowing good and evil? This is the idea of the tower of babble, the WEF, UN, etc. But no one can unseat God from his throne!

Every day, the eyes of God move too and fro, watching our actions, seeing if any are willing to stand in the gap. We need to be that people, for the world does as it pleases, and they reduce the poor and weak to food tickets, bargaining chips, and things for sport. They take advantage, they murder and plunder, without regard for the heart or soul.

I live by grace by faith; and by faith that God would bless the few loaves and fishes did he feed five thousand men, and also women and children. Jesus said we would do even greater things, so let's begin to have a heart that wants to clean up our workplaces, our governmental leaders, and lead the way!

1 PETER 1: 14 - 20

As obedient children, do not conform to the evil desires you had when you lived in ignorance. 15 But just as he who called you is holy, so be holy in all you do; 16 for it is written: "Be holy, because I am holy." 17 Since you call on a Father who judges each person's work impartially, live out your time as foreigners here in reverent fear.

A. Do Not Love this Life

Read John 12: 23 – 26

Read 2 Corinthians 5: 5 – 9

Read 1 John 3: 20 – 23

> 1 JOHN 2: 15
>
> *Do not love the world or the things in the world. If anyone loves the world, the love of the Father is not in him.*

Prayer

Lord, help us to see the difference between being light and life in Jesus Christ, versus chasing the pride and blind ambitions and lusts of the flesh that so many in our world follow. Like Christ, the man/woman must die, and your Spirit must be born within. Give us the love of Jesus and the faith of a mustard seed, that we will produce 60 or 100-fold through this life, showing people something they have never seen, so that they may ask us where our confidence comes from, and we may point them to you. When we want what you want, and you give it to us, we know that you love us, and others will see it too, so let us love you more than anything this world can offer, in Jesus' name, amen.

FOR DEEPER STUDY:

John 12 • 2 Corinthians • 1 John 2, 3

B. Spiritual Riches

Read Ephesians 3: 8 – 12

Read Colossians 2: 1 – 4

Read Revelation 5: 11 – 13

> LUKE 12: 29
>
> *And do not seek what you should eat or what you should drink, nor have an anxious mind.*

Prayer

Father, may we see ourselves and those you want us to reach as the riches of your kingdom. Help us to use every means available upon this earth to secure the souls of your people, and share in our inheritance after this life, at that great reunion in heaven! May we grow daily in our thirst for your knowledge and understanding, and love of you and one another. The earthly mind values riches and demoralizes and demeans humanity, but thanks be to you that you have a better way, and I pray to see the day when I will lay my riches at your feet, and instead, long to remain where you are. Listening to your words that bring life! Amen.

FOR DEEPER STUDY:

Luke 12 • Ephesians 3 • Colossians 2 • Revelation 5

C. Flee Temptation

Read Genesis 19: 17 – 20

Read 1 Corinthians 10: 12 – 14

Read 2 Peter 2: 4 – 9

JAMES 1: 17

Every good gift and every perfect gift is from above, and comes down from the Father of lights, with whom there is no variation or shadow of turning.

Prayer

May we not misuse these giftings and opportunities you give for us to lead others to you. We are to be in the world, but not of the world. Let no destruction come near our tent, so all may see you at work, when danger strikes. Make us stronger than temptation, or lead us yourself in the direction of escape. We know that the destruction and judgment of the fallen is sure, along with all who follow their ways. Like Noah and Lot, may we be an example that others will see you at work, and give you all the praise and exaltation for making all see this. The greatest of these gifts is your Son, who made it possible for us to be reconciled to you.

FOR DEEPER STUDY:

Genesis 19 • 1 Corinthians 10 • James 1 • 2 Peter 2

D. Eternal Word/Love

Read Matthew John 1: 1 – 9

Read John 6: 66 – 69

Read Romans 1: 15 – 17

MARK 8: 38

For whoever is ashamed of Me and My words in this adulterous and sinful generation, of him, the Son of Man, also will be ashamed when He comes in the glory of His Father with the holy angels.

Prayer

Father, we have been here with you since the beginning, and just like your words to us, your love for us is forever! You spoke the world into existence, this by itself is mind blowing, you commanded us to live in and take care of your world. Though we sinned and have corrupted it, your love remains, and you demonstrated it by bringing Jesus to earth to live, die, and live again, and join you in heaven so that we may too. Grant us gracious, thankful unashamed hearts overflowing with love sharing this message, showing love for you and each other.

FOR DEEPER STUDY:

Matthew 24 • Mark 8 • John 1, 6 • Romans 1

E. Living With Him

Read Romans 6: 7 – 9

Read 1 Thessalonians 5: 9 – 11

Read Revelation 20: 3 – 4

GALATIANS 2: 20

I have been crucified with Christ; it is no longer I who live, but Christ lives in me; and the life which I now live in the flesh I live by faith in the Son of God, who loved me and gave Himself for me.

Prayer

Father, we want to live, breathe, thrive, and have joy, seeing your face, and living in the light of your grace. Let your spirit flood us with your words, so that we may hear, believe, live and share them with all the world to hear. May we also raise your name to the heavens, so that the world will see you moving, and believe on your name. Remove all fear, doubt, uncertainty, and discouragement. For you give us a Spirit of power, love and a sound mind. From now on, we live for you, and one day we will live with you, in heaven. Amen.

FOR DEEPER STUDY:

Romans 6 • 1 Thessalonians 5 • 2 Timothy 1 • Galatians 2 • Revelation 20

F. Obedience Rewarded

Read Deuteronomy 11: 1 – 5

Read Psalm 19: 7 – 11

Read Luke 6: 34 – 36

> MATTHEW 25: 23
>
> *His lord said to him, 'Well done, good and faithful servant; you have been faithful over a few things, I will make you ruler over many things. Enter into the joy of your lord.'*

Prayer

Father, if there is any opportunity for us to look back on all our lives, whether good or bad, we will see you there, through the pain and struggles, the trials, tears, and sleepless nights. Teach us to prize your word and your commands, that our words and behaviors will lead others to salvation in you. Make us truthful, and may we seek a crown that will never fade, an inheritance that will never tarnish or get old. Help us to use riches wisely, to influence and assist others and show them that there is a God in which we hope and have faith. In Jesus name, amen.

FOR DEEPER STUDY:

Deuteronomy 11 • Psalm 19 • Matthew 25 • Luke 6

G. Talented (Gifted)

Read Exodus 31: 1 – 6

Read 1 Corinthians 12: 4 – 10

Read 2 Timothy 3: 10 – 12

> 2 CORINTHIANS 9: 8
>
> *And God is able to make all grace abound toward you, that you, always having all sufficiency in all things, may have an abundance for every good work.*

Prayer

Thank you, father for abilities, gifts of every kind that make life meaningful, and Spiritual Gifts that produce fruit, took Moses of the Nile and made him a Prince of Egypt, and a leader and elder of Israel, bringing them to the place where they could meet with you and, with the help of skilled labourers, made a tabernacle. May we be as diligent, preparing our hearts, souls, and minds for your Spirit to dwell as we begin to live and grow in you. Make us strong enough to withstand persecution, and not cave in to the world's demands. Grant us an extra helping of your grace, so we may do all things through Christ who strengthens us.

FOR DEEPER STUDY:

Exodus 31 • 1 Corinthians 12 • 2 Corinthians 9 • 2 Timothy 3

H. Countenance of Light

Read Exodus 34: 25 – 35

Read Numbers 6: 22 – 27

Read Matthew 5: 13 – 15

PHILIPPIANS 2: 15

that you may become blameless and[c]harmless, children of God without fault in the midst of a crooked and perverse generation, among whom you shine as lights in the world.

Prayer

Father, let your light in, until we are bathed, removing our fear, shame, your light shines on us, showing you to be right there next to us, as you were with Moses when you spoke your words to him. Shine your face on us and be gracious to us, gently lifting us from the soot and smoke, and wiping us clean. Have your angels clothe us in clean clothes, and give us peace, knowing you are with us wherever we go. Help us to be like a lighthouse, not warning of danger, but drawing all to you, and showing that our countenance is like yours, so they may feel safe, and draw closer to you. As your light spreads, may we expose darkness, and show the light to be greater. Amen.

FOR DEEPER STUDY:

Exodus 34 • Numbers 6 • Matthew 5 • Philippians 2

I. Rooted & Abounding

Read Mark 4: 16 – 20

Read 2 Corinthians 1: 3 – 6

Read Philippians 1: 8 – 11

COLOSSIANS 2: 7

Rooted and built up in Him and established in the faith, as you have been taught, abounding in it with thanksgiving.

Prayer

Father, being covered in corruption and immortality sounds good, but being rooted in you sounds even better, for on our own we cannot produce anything! We are selfish, sinful, and hurtful; give us love, compassion, and resolve to live and care for others. Every word, action, and prayer should be a seed you have sowed, make the ground fertile to receive your word, and us eager and grateful to do the work of harvesting. Plant in us the fruit of righteousness, and when trouble abounds, may our comfort and joy abound as well. Keep our minds rooted in you, as your word leads us in exponential growth, and joy inexpressible. In Jesus' name, we pray, Amen.

FOR DEEPER STUDY:

Mark 4 • 1 Corinthians 15 • 2 Corinthians 1, 9 • Philippians 1 • Colossians 2

J. Team Players

Read Romans 15: 5 – 7

Read Ephesians 4: 11 – 13

Read 1 Thessalonians 5: 14 – 18

> 2 CORINTHIANS 9: 10– 13
>
> *Because of the service by which you have proved yourselves, others will praise God for the obedience that accompanies your confession of the gospel of Christ, and for your generosity in sharing with them and with everyone else.*

Prayer

Give us the mind of Christ, who did not consider equality with you but keep us humble to do your will. May this give us endurance and encouragement in times of trial and tribulation. Unity in love, grace, and compassion, building up one another and showing you to be real in our world should be the goal, using our gifts so that the world lets go of the things that give them a false sense of hope and grab hold of you. Our heartfelt thanksgiving and our service will show that we are commanded by one who loves all and wants all to love you. Amen.

FOR DEEPER STUDY:

Romans 5 • 2 Corinthians 9 • Ephesians 3 • 1 Thessalonians 5

CHAPTER 14

ANCHORED

(One Goal, Love)

Psalm 112 • Zechariah 8 • Hebrews 6

So many analogies to shifting shadows, mire, and mud, depths, and rock. In Genesis, the earth was formless and empty. Darkness was over the surface of the deep. David told us that to God even the darkness is light, Moses had to veil his face after being with God because it shone, and when we do good, our light is seen. We will dwell secure in our faith in the one who walks with us!

When Solomon completed the Temple, God spoke, not just to him, but all Jerusalem, making it clear that in humility of self, and repentance from evil, would allow our prayers to go heavenward and render a response from Him.

We long to live a life that shows something of promise. This cannot be done so long as the motive or result is to puff ourself up, but when Christ Jesus is lifted up, we too are exulted, and others will take this to heart, and want what we've got. In this message from Isaiah, the remnant in Israel were praised as the ones in whom God called living branches. This includes us.

HEBREWS 6: 17 - 19

Because God wanted to make the unchanging nature of his purpose very clear to the heirs of what was promised, he confirmed it with an oath. 18 God did this so that, by two unchangeable things in which it is impossible for God to lie, we who have fled to take hold of the hope set before us may be greatly encouraged. 19 We have this hope as an anchor for the soul, firm and secure. It enters the inner sanctuary behind the curtain.

A. Abiding Faith

Read Psalm 91: 1 – 3

Read John 15: 4 – 7

Read 1 John 2: 14 – 17

HEBREWS 12: 1

Therefore, we also, since we are surrounded by so great a cloud of witnesses, let us lay aside every weight, and the sin which so easily ensnares us, and let us run with endurance the race that is set before us.

Prayer

Abide in me is a favorite song, but it is also a call that shows that we're disturbed by this world and need the safety that you offer. With all the comforts this world can offer, may we see your word, and your ways priceless in comparison. All we do means nothing unless you lead and direct it, so may we abide in you and enjoy being a blessing to all. Give us heart and mind stayed on eternity, and your ways. As followers, we are on display, so help us to stay strong and clear in the way forward, and the strength that comes from your word and your Spirit, in Jesus' name we pray, amen.

FOR DEEPER STUDY:

Psalm 91 • John 5 • Hebrews 11, 12 • 1 John 2

B. Binding & Loosing

Read Psalm 56: 10 – 13

Read Matthew 16: 17 – 19

Read Matthew 18: 18 – 22

NUMBERS 30: 2

If a man makes a vow to the Lord, or swears an oath to bind himself by some agreement, he shall not break his word; he shall do according to all that proceeds out of his mouth.

Prayer

Thank you, father, that you set this law up at the get go. You told Abraham to move from Haran to Canaan and promised you would make him the father of nations. Your vow was binding, and so it is that accepting Christ and obeying you is binding, when we do not act in your will or ways, it serves the enemy. Thank you for giving the church (your bride) the authority to bind and loose, (on earth and in heaven) this give The Lord's prayer new meaning for me, and also the prayers of married couples who care for their families and serve your people. Help this knowledge to move us forward in confidence to do good, in Jesus' name, amen.

FOR DEEPER STUDY:

Numbers 30 • Psalm 56 • Matthew 16, 18

C. Persistent in Prayer

Read Luke 18: 1 – 3

Read Romans 12: 8 – 13

Read 1 Thessalonians 5: 14 – 18

REVELATION 8: 3

Then another angel, having a golden censer, came and stood at the altar. He was given much incense, that he should offer it with the prayers of all the saints upon the golden altar which was before the throne.

Prayer

We pray that you might make more people more open to receiving the pleas of the oppressed and hurting as it seems many in power abuse it and appear self interested. Help us to keep the greatest commandment in mind when preparing for prayer, offering thanksgiving to you for all you promise to do in your word, and petitioning you for our needs and others needs. Help us to fan into flame the Spirit within us, ignoring worldly pursuits, and showing concern for and giving help to those who are in need. Grant us a willing Spirit to exalt you and each other, and provide help and hope to all. In Jesus' name, Amen.

FOR DEEPER STUDY:

Luke 18 • Romans 12 • 1 Thessalonians 5 • Revelation 8

D. Unfailing Love

Read John 15: 12 – 14

Read 1 Corinthians 13: 4 – 8

Read Revelation 21: 2 – 4

JOHN 3: 17

For God did not send His Son into the world to condemn the world, but that the world through Him might be saved.

Prayer

Father, throughout history the evidence of your love is seen, in rescuing Lot and his family, the Israelites from Egypt, and the deposition of nations in Canaan. Though the nations people did not love you, and mistreated their own, you show yourself loving. May we take Jesus' example, in the Greatest Commandment, and the Apostle Paul's explanation of what love is and is not. When everything else in this world fails, let your love be seen in all we say and do! When the world becomes less loving, may your Spirit strengthen the love that remains in us, so all may be drawn to you. In Jesus' name, Amen.

FOR DEEPER STUDY:

John 3, 15 • 1 Corinthians 13 • Revelation 21

E. Set an Example

Read John 13: 13 – 15

Read 1 Timothy 4: 12 – 14

Read Titus 2: 11 – 15

JAMES 5: 11

Indeed we count them blessed who endure. You have heard of the perseverance of Job and seen the end intended by the Lord—that the Lord is very compassionate and merciful.

Prayer

Thank you, Father, for sending Abraham, Job, the Prophets, Jesus and the apostles, as examples for us to pattern our life after. Just as the teacher showed us, so let us be servants to the world around us, showing love, being patient, and showing that you are our master. Make our conduct faithful, lovely, and pure, bringing a breath of fresh air, and a feeling of hope to all who are struggling today. Increase in us the giftings you gave us, let no temptation overtake us, and no problem make us anxious. Purify us daily from wrong ideas or actions, may we, like you, show mercy and love, and persevere amidst trials, proving you are stronger than any circumstance. In Jesus' name, Amen.

FOR DEEPER STUDY:

John 13 • 1 Timothy 4 • James 5 • Titus 2

F. Asking Confidently

Read Matthew 7: 7 – 11

Read James 1: 5 – 8

Read 1 John 5: 14 – 16

HEBREWS 3: 14

For we have become partakers of Christ if we hold the beginning of our confidence steadfast to the end.

Prayer

Father, your son Jesus reminded us that you are good, giving to all who ask and believe in you. In confidence and strength, seeking your will, and filled with all joy, let us move forward, toward you, asking for the tools to succeed in your plans! You who gives good things, may we believe that you would never sell us short, show us your joy and renew our strength, that we may see you working through us to achieve your aims. Let nothing blind us to the truth that you are God and you will deliver what you have promised. Let our thanksgivings, praise, and petitions bring you joy as you make every answer YES and AMEN!

FOR DEEPER STUDY:

Matthew 7 • Hebrews 3 • James 1 • 1 John 5

G. His Strength in Our Weakness

Read Romans 8: 24 – 26

Read 1 Corinthians 1: 27 – 29

Read 2 Corinthians 12: 7 – 10

PSALM 18: 1 – 2

I will love You, O Lord, my strength. The Lord is my rock and my fortress and my deliverer; My God, my strength, in whom I will trust; My shield and the horn of my salvation, my stronghold.

Prayer

Father, as human beings, we are weak, contemptible, corruptible, and our death in this form is inevitable. But, in the Spirit, we are alive, and you have made this possible. The Fallen angels know this and they know that their doom is sure. Like Abraham, we cannot see the future, but we believe you will finish what you start, so we have faith that will weather this life and bring us into the next! We glory in our weakness, knowing that your strength in the Spirit is the only way forward. Let our love for and appreciation of you be eternal. This we pray in Jesus' name, amen

FOR DEEPER STUDY:

Psalm 18 • Romans 8 • 1 Corinthians 1 • 2 Corinthians 12

H. Confident in Hope

Read Psalm 27: 10 – 14

Read 2 Corinthians 6: 5 – 9

Read 1 John 2: 27 – 29

> PHILIPPIANS 1: 14
>
> *And because of my chains, most of the brothers and sisters have become confident in the Lord and dare all the more to proclaim the gospel without fear.*

Prayer

Lead us in your paths of righteousness for your namesake, that even those who oppress and deceive may see that your way is best and most peaceful even for them. Help us to see our purpose in you, on earth and for eternity, shining like stars, and guiding others to you. May our faith, small as a mustard seed, blossom, and grow into something that is beautiful and useful, leading others to want this for themselves. May our plans and dreams be pleasing in your eyes. May we act as children of the living God, regardless of the cunning of the enemy, and their perceived strength, may we show the world that you are stronger, brighter, and the only on in which to put our confidence. Amen

FOR DEEPER STUDY:

Psalm 27, 106 • 2 Corinthians 6 • Philippians 1 • 1 John 2

I. Compassionate & Forgiving

Read Nehemiah 9: 16 – 17

Read Psalm 145: 8 – 13

Read Ephesians 4: 29 – 32

> COLOSSIANS 3: 13
>
> *...bearing with one another, and forgiving one another, if anyone has a complaint against another; even as Christ forgave you, so you also must do.*

Prayer

Lord, sometimes the actions and words of others leave us jaded, hurt, anxious, and upset, it seems like building walls is a better way to insulate ourselves and stay safe. But you call on us to forgive and forget, to return good for evil, to show compassion and understanding. In doing so, we see that we are able to not only heal, but change our perceptions of the people and world around us, increasing our faith in you! No keeping score, no times tables to memorize, only the continuing debt to love one another. What an amazing way to show the enemy they are defeated!

FOR DEEPER STUDY:

Nehemiah 9 • Psalm 145 • Matthew 18 • Ephesians 4 • Colossians 3

J. Contend for the Faith

Read Genesis 32: 25 – 28

Read Ecclesiastes 6: 9 – 11

Read Colossians 1: 26 – 29

JUDE 1: 3 – 4

Beloved, while I was very diligent to write to you concerning our common salvation, I found it necessary to write to you exhorting you to contend earnestly for the faith which was once for all delivered to the saints.

Prayer

Father, help us to see that our striving for the faith is not a losing battle. When I was young, I didn't understand that I had to work to attain faith, just as my parents gave me things, I figured you'd give me this, also. When that didn't happen, I began to doubt because I didn't understand. Jacob wrestled with Laban and you, we face our goliaths in life, and we must believe you will lead us to victory. Help us to wrestle daily with forces seen and unseen, to deliver the gospel to the world, with the strength God gives us all.

FOR DEEPER STUDY:

Genesis 32 • Ecclesiastes 6 • Colossians 1 • Jude 1

CHAPTER 15

ENDURING

(Participating in Faith)

Galatians 6 • Philippians 1 • 1 Peter 3

Patience, they say, is a virtue. This has been especially true in my life! Even to non-believers, I share that we are learning our entire lives, and each day I'm challenged to do something different. But we are also aware of the life we once lived when we served ourself, and in fact, we were serving the evil one. In helping others to see who we were and now are, and sharing their burdens helps us to do the will of the Father.

Not only are our actions being witnessed, but we are called upon to test our own actions so that we can be confident of our place in the family of God! Our conduct and our striving are seen by God, angels, and humanity, in this our faith is shown to be something that will surpass everything our world has to offer! We will suffer much, but we will see the glory of God, and meet Him face to face! What a wonderful meeting that will be, and we will know and understand each others words and actions.

1 PETER 3: 14 - 17

But even if you should suffer for what is right, you are blessed. "Do not fear their threats; do not be frightened." But in your hearts revere Christ as Lord. Always be prepared to give an answer to everyone who asks you to give the reason for the hope that you have. But do this with gentleness and respect, keeping a clear conscience, so that those who speak maliciously against your good behavior in Christ may be ashamed of their slander. For it is better, if it is God's will, to suffer for doing good than for doing evil.

A. Good News

Read Matthew 9: 35 – 38

Read Acts 11: 19 – 21

Read Hebrews 4: 10 – 13

ISAIAH 52: 7

How beautiful upon the mountains are the feet of him who brings good news, who proclaims peace, who brings glad tidings of good things, who proclaims salvation, who says to Zion, "Your God reigns!'

Prayer

Father, may we rejoice and gain strength in your presence as we tell the world the good news that you have saved us, we need only accept this and believe it to be saved. We pray that just as in the days of Jesus, we would have His power to speak boldly, to heal disease and sickness, and show that there is someone in whom to place our hope. We know that opposition will come, show us when to stand our ground, and when you are sending us elsewhere because our world is hungry for this news. Grant that the word of the Lord that we speak may reach the hearts and minds of all and bless us for speaking the truth in love and grace. Amen.

FOR DEEPER STUDY:

Isaiah 52 • Matthew 9 • Acts 11 • Hebrews 3, 4

B. Bear One Another's Burdens

Read Isaiah 58: 5 – 7

Read Romans 15: 5 – 8

Read Ephesians 4: 1 – 6

> GALATIANS 6: 2
>
> *Bear one another's burdens, and in so doing, fulfill the law of Christ.*

Prayer

Help us, Father, to fast from self, and become selfless, seeing to the needs, concerns, and obstacles facing others. Help us to see beyond words and behaviors, and take time to get to know those around us, instead of just insisting on our wants. Give us the mind of Christ, who gave of himself in order to lift others, so they stood together, giving praise to you. Whatever blessings and opportunities we receive in life, may we remain humble, gentle, and loving. Grant us a Spirit of unity, that we may continually care for one another, and help one another when we are down, or facing difficulties of every kind. In Jesus' name, Amen.

FOR DEEPER STUDY:

Isaiah 58 • Romans 15 • Galatians 6 • Ephesians 4

C. Light of Life

Read Psalm 27: 1 – 4

Read John 1 – 7

Read 2 Timothy 1: 9 – 14

PSALM 27: 1

The Lord is my light and my salvation;
who shall I fear? The Lord is the strength of my life;
Of whom shall I be afraid?

Prayer

Light of the world, you spoke us into being, a few thousand years later, Jesus entered the world and once more a light was cast, on your word, your commands, and your people! Not every one of my deeds is light, they are impure, but when we stumble, you keep us from falling too far. Let this calm assurance keep us moving in the light of your grace and truth. As your word continues to be read, let it seep into every crack and crevice of our lives showing us where we need to give up wrong things and embrace your will for our lives. Nothing is dark to you, and you will never leave us or forsake us.

FOR DEEPER STUDY:

Psalm 27, 139 • John 1 • 2 Timothy 1

D. Bearing Witness

Read John 1: 7 – 9

Read Romans 8: 13 – 17

Read 1 John 1: 1 – 5

> 1 JOHN 5: 6
>
> *This is He who came by water and blood—Jesus Christ; not only by water, but by water and blood. And it is the Spirit who bears witness, because the Spirit is truth.*

Prayer

Thank you, Lord, for establishing on the earth witnesses and disciples. They were faithful in the things you gave them to do. Help us, like the disciples, to learn to die to ourselves and let your Holy Spirit lead, guide, and direct us in all our ways so that all may see that we are indeed your children. Some who are bearing witness, see that miracle even now. We long for the life to come, and wait in eager expectation, but many are blind to what has taken place, help us to bring the good news of Jesus to light in the lives of all. Amen.

FOR DEEPER STUDY:

John 1 • Romans 8 • 1 John 1

E. Remain Unified in Christ

Read John 15: 13 – 16

Read 1 Thessalonians 4: 15 – 18

Read Hebrews 12: 25 – 29

> 1 CORINTHIANS 1: 10
>
> *Now I plead with you, brethren, by the name of our Lord Jesus Christ, that you all speak the same thing, and that there be no divisions among you, but that you be perfectly joined together in mind and judgment.*

Prayer

Father, these actions of laying down our life, and yet remaining in you, require stretching, and relying evermore on your Spirit. Give us one mind, voice, and goal, Love. Let our conduct be pure, above reproach, pure, gentle, but firm, and concise, so there will be no dichotomy in thought, word or deed. For we are all your children, and you chose us, so no one is above another. Grant us peace, hope, and strength, and may what we do, in your name, be seen clearly by all as the exaltation of your name, with hearts full of gratitude and praise, and devoid of darkness, sin, or hatred. Amen.

FOR DEEPER STUDY:

John 15 • 1 Corinthians 1 • 1 Thessalonians 4 • Hebrews 12

F. Complex Wisdom

Read Psalm 104: 27 - 30

Read Ephesians 3: 14 – 19

Read 2 Peter 4: 14 – 18

> 1 CORINTHIANS 1: 21
>
> *For since, in the wisdom of God, the world through wisdom did not know God, it pleased God through the foolishness of the message preached to save those who believe.*

Prayer

Father, we're often absorbed in self struggle, fleshly pursuits, and problems caused by sin, or Spiritual interference. Grant us the serenity to accept what we can't control, courage to change the things we can, and wisdom to discern between the two. Jesus did what no one before or since has been able to do for each and every one of us. Over 2000 years ago, Immanuel (God with us became a reality) and though Jesus ascended to join you, he is still within our heart, mind and soul, and avails Himself to all who believe and receive. Purify us, so you can present us to yourself on that day, as true children. Amen.

FOR DEEPER STUDY:

Psalm 104 • 1 Corinthians 1 • Ephesians 3 • 2 Peter 4

G. Spiritually Gifted to Serve & Share

Read Romans 12: 1 – 21

Read 1 Corinthians 1: 26 – 29

Read 2 Timothy 1: 8 – 10

> 2 THESSALONIANS 1: 11
>
> *Therefore, we also pray always for you that our God would count you worthy of His calling, and fulfill all the good pleasure of His goodness and the work of faith with power.*

Prayer

Father, as priests in Moses' day, daily sacrificed for the sins of the people, so shall our lives be a sacrifice to you, so that our conduct maybe pleasing as the aroma you smelled in the wilderness. Let our lives, our hearts and our Spirits be changed, and that of the people around us. Remind us that like Abram, you called us, while in the amidst of our sin and affliction, and lifted us from the filth, chosen over the rich and powerful, to influence all who would believe in you. May our zeal to share you with the world around us mirror your promise to never leave or forsake us. May we rejoice that you invite us to join in spreading the good news. Amen.

FOR DEEPER STUDY:

1 Samuel 16 • Romans 12 • 1 Corinthians 1 • 2 Thessalonians 1 • 2 Timothy 1

H. Confess Your Sins

Read Proverbs 28: 10 – 14

Read James 5: 16 – 18

Read 1 John 1: 6 – 10

> 2 CORINTHIANS 5: 20
>
> *Now then, we are ambassadors for Christ, as though God were pleading through us: we implore you, on Christ's behalf, be reconciled to God.*

Prayer

We remember that his sacrifice was one time for all our sin, and you have forgiven us, so too let us forgive our brother and sister from our heart. Help us to confess our sin and ask for mercy. So many burdened and afflicted souls are crying out or giving up hope of getting out from underneath, but help us to walk away from these by confessing and renouncing them. Grant us humble and merciful hearts that are forgiving, patient, and servant minded. Help us to walk in the light of your word, with your Spirit leading all we say and do, Jesus being the example we should follow. This conduct will show us to be your children, and ambassadors for you. In Jesus' name we pray, Amen.

FOR DEEPER STUDY:

Proverbs 28 • 2 Corinthians 5 • James 5 • 1 John 1

I. As Iron Sharpens Iron

Read Proverbs 27: 17 – 21

Read 2 Corinthians 10: 14 – 18

Read Galatians 6: 6 – 10

COLOSSIANS 3: 16

Let the word of Christ dwell in you richly in all wisdom, teaching and admonishing one another in psalms and hymns and spiritual songs, singing with grace in your hearts to the Lord.

Prayer

Father, we know we're rough around the edges, and are being made new, lifting you high. Grant us the strength to show your goodness to all and preach the news that Jesus saves to all. Give us all that we need to live, and give us rest so we are refreshed to do it each day that you lend us breath. May your word and Spirit lead and direct our thoughts, words, and deeds, so that no one is offended and we do not lead anyone astray. You have put eternity in our hearts, help us to convey that in YOU only can it be attained, and enjoyed. Grace us with joyful and peaceful hearts as we share all these things with all people.

FOR DEEPER STUDY:

Proverbs 27 • 2 Corinthians 10 • Galatians 6 • Colossians 3

J. Forgive One Another

Read 2 Corinthians 2: 3 – 17

Read James 5: 14 – 16

Read 1 John 1: 7 – 10

LUKE 17: 3

Take heed to yourselves. If your brother sins against you, rebuke him; and if he repents, forgive him.

Prayer

Father, forgive us for things done or said that offend you and those around us. In the world today we see so much oppression, greed, distress, depression, apprehension, and hurt. Help us to bring the aroma of life to our world, not some useless and greed driven agenda, but life in Christ! Make us conduits of prayer, faith, healing, and life, comforting all who are in need, and forgiving sins, opening doors to understanding and compassion. Forgive us when we do not walk in your light and call us back lovingly. Help us to not keep track of offences, but to forgive as you have forgiven us. In Jesus' name, amen.

FOR DEEPER STUDY:

Luke 17 • 2 Corinthians 2 • James 5 • 1 John 1

CHAPTER 16

FAMILY

(One church)

Ephesians 4 • Colossians 1 • Colossians 3

During his many travels, Paul became an effective letter writer. I wonder what it might have been like to have him for a pen pal! His letters to the churches, more than this journeys to the churches he founded with many helpers, is remembered and documented throughout the New Testament. Paul was not one of the 12 who walked, talked, and witnessed the miracles, and deeds, and death and resurrection of Jesus Christ, but he met him when he was blinded.

We are children of the life, and God has given us Spiritual gifts so that we can accomplish His will, and show ourselves to be his. Jesus promised these and said that we would do equally amazing things and even greater ones. We cannot remain hiding in buildings, but we are called to build up the church and exalt His name, so all might bend the knee and confess He is Lord. What is the measure of the fullness of Christ? Who's ready to find out? This will be more than a wild ride, but it is what we are called to.

COLOSSIANS 3: 15 - 17

Let the peace of Christ rule in your hearts, since as members of one body you were called to peace.And be thankful. 16Let the message of Christ dwell among you richly as you teach and admonish one another with all wisdom through psalms, hymns, and songs from the Spirit, singing to God with gratitude in your hearts. 17And whatever you do, whether in word or deed, do it all in the name of the Lord Jesus, giving thanks to God the Father through him.

A. Ordered to Build Up

Read Isaiah 57: 14 – 16

Read Luke 18: 9 – 30

Read Philippians 1: 12 – 14

ISAIAH 54: 2

Enlarge the place of your tent, and let them stretch out the curtains of your dwellings; Do not spare; Lengthen your cords, and strengthen your stakes.

Prayer

Father, grant us willing hearts to build up your church, to make clear the way to you, and remove any physical, mental or Spiritual obstacle to becoming your children. May our sins not condemn us, but let our humbleness of heart, and heart of love welcome in all who call to you to be saved. Help us to leave the safe and familiar, to traverse new ground, challenge the world's norms, and show others that only with you can anything good happen! Many live under oppression in prison, or as enemies of the state, but those who believe, give thanks to you for showing us all a way to life everlasting, and joy in you. Help us to open our minds, our hearts, and places of worship, for all you will do. Amen.

FOR DEEPER STUDY:

Isaiah 54, 57, 58 • Luke 18 • Philippians 1

B. This Do in Remembrance

Read Luke 22: 16 – 20

Read John 14: 23 – 27

Read 1 Corinthians 11: 23 – 26

> 2 CORINTHIANS 3: 18
>
> *But we all, with unveiled face, beholding as in a mirror the glory of the Lord, are being transformed into the same image from glory to glory, just as by the Spirit of the Lord.*

Prayer

Father, we thank you for having Jesus institute the Lord's Supper. May every meal whether we eat it alone, or with family or strangers be a remembrance of you and anticipation of us eating together. We long to come home and embrace. Just as eating and drinking is essential to life, may we see you, and your word, and your son's work. Let us also share this with all who will sup with us so that they will be immersed in the love and knowledge of the one who loves them. Amen.

FOR DEEPER STUDY:

Luke 22 • John 14 • 1 Corinthians 11 • 2 Corinthians 3

C. Foundation of Rock

Read Psalm 40: 1 – 3

Read Psalm 118: 22 – 26

Read Matthew 16: 16 – 19

ACTS 2: 25

For David says concerning Him: "I foresaw the Lord always before my face, For He is at my right hand, that I may not be shaken."

Prayer

Father, we struggle to seek your will and ways, many fail to see significance in this life, reassure us that in love you pulled us from the chaos of the depths of destruction. Grant us grateful, thankful, humbled, and kind hearts to all who are facing similar situations. You lifted me onto a stone, and called the church your rock, may all who are confused, upset, oppressed, and distressed come to your church, and may we, the body, supply their needs in Christ Jesus, and point them toward you, as we continue to be a place of refuge, peace, rest, and significance in a world devoid of these. Amen.

FOR DEEPER STUDY:

Psalm 40 • Psalm 118 • Matthew 16 • Acts 2

D. Light for Our Path

Read Psalm 27: 1 – 4

Read Psalm 119: 105 – 109

Read 2 Corinthians 4: 16 – 18

MATTHEW 5: 16

Let your light so shine before men, that they may see your good works and glorify your Father in heaven.

Prayer

Father, many of us yearn for times when a light bulb goes on in our minds, an aha, or a moment of recognizing something good. Make us intrepid to all who are against your agenda, because they will know without a doubt that you go with us everywhere we put our foot. Help us to see that there is no place where you are not present, and your light gives life to all who call you daddy. Help us to stand firm in our faith in you, standing out like lighthouses in this dark world. Let our lives be daily sacrificed for you to show the world your love, truth, wisdom, and will for them. This we ask in Jesus' name, Amen.

FOR DEEPER STUDY:

Psalm 27, 19, 139 • Matthew 5 • 2 Corinthians 4

E. Grateful Hearts of Thanks

Read Nehemiah 12: 27 – 30

Read Psalm 100: 1 – 5

Read 2 Corinthians 9: 8 – 11

> COLOSSIANS 3: 16
>
> *Let the word of Christ dwell in you richly in all wisdom, teaching, and admonishing one another in psalms, and hymns, and spiritual songs, singing with grace in your hearts to the Lord.*

Prayer

Father, we have a new reason to rejoice, Immanuel, "God with us" is made possible in the promised Holy Spirit. Let us see this gift for what it is, and be grateful that your perfect plan included making daily sacrifice and repentance one in the same! Help us to purify ourselves from the world's filth so we will not be found to be comfortable with it. Lead us as a shepherd, as David said, and give us peace, joy, and fitting rest in their time. Make us gracious and overflow with joy in you with our giving, knowing that you love us and will supply all our needs in Christ Jesus. Amen.

FOR DEEPER STUDY:

Nehemiah 12 • Psalm 100 • 2 Corinthians 9 • Colossians 2

F. The Great Commission

Read Matthew 11: 10 – 15

Read Mark 18: 14 – 18

Read 1 Peter 4: 7 – 11

> JOSHUA 1: 9
>
> *Have I not commanded you? Be strong and of good courage; do not be afraid, nor be dismayed, for the Lord your God is with you wherever you go!*

Prayer

Father, thank you for sending us. Your Son has gone before us as an example, and your Spirit is within, and you promise to never leave or forsake us. John prepared the way as he was instructed. Jesus did many great things and even spoke in his own town of the prophesies of Isaiah. He would ordain the disciples, as he does us now to go into the world and spread the news of all you have done. Give us the authority of Jesus to cast out demons, speak in tongues, heal the sick, and survive deadly ills. Grant us that fire in our belly to use our gift to the best of our ability to reach all, bringing them to you. In Jesus' name, Amen.

FOR DEEPER STUDY:

Joshua 1 • Matthew 11 • Mark 18 • 1 Peter 4

G. Iron & Discipleship

Read Psalm 94: 10 – 14

Read Proverbs 3: 7 – 12

Read Hebrews 12: 5 – 8

HEBREWS 12: 1

Therefore, we also, since we are surrounded by so great a cloud of witnesses, let us lay aside every weight, and the sin which so easily ensnares us, and let us run with endurance the race that is set before us.

Prayer

Father, Help us to see that it is not about us, but about you and everyone else. Show us that despite the things in your creation, you are more important than comforts, riches, pleasures, and conquests. Grant us hearts and minds that crave your wisdom over our own, may we give generously of a grateful heart, and be blessed for all we do, let us welcome your discipline, so that we grow into full maturity as believers. Remind us that we live our lives not alone, but being seen for who we are and what we do, by humanity and angels, in heaven and on earth, so let us act in accordance with your will. For Jesus' sake, amen.

FOR DEEPER STUDY:

Psalm 94 • Proverbs 3, 27 • Hebrews 12

H. Celebrating Joy, Diversity, & Maturity

Read Proverbs 8: 27 – 31

Read Luke 15: 8 – 10

Read 2 Corinthians 6: 6 – 10

> 1 CORINTHIANS 13: 3
>
> *And though I bestow all my goods to feed the poor, and though I give my body to be burned, but have not love, it profits me nothing.*

Prayer

Thank you, Father. You told us never will I leave you and never will I forsake you; you've been with us ever since you made us and ordained our days of life, every page of your book records our lives and deeds. We pray that it would read like a song of praise for the ways we are different from each other, and how your works are displayed through our lives. As you sought us when we were lost, make us tireless in our pursuit of brothers, sisters, children and friends who are lost. Purify our hearts, giving us eyes, hearts, and mouths that are brimming with love, praise, compassion and love, for Jesus' sake, Amen.

FOR DEEPER STUDY:

Psalm 139 • Proverbs 8 • Luke 15 • 1 Corinthians 13 • 2 Corinthians 6 • Hebrews 13

I. Sabbath Rest, Make Sure You Are Ready

Read Deuteronomy 5: 12 – 14

Read Matthew 25: 1 – 5

Read Philippians 1: 27 – 28

EPHESIANS 5: 16

...redeeming the time, because the days are evil.

Prayer

Father, let none of our actions unnecessarily make others work. Work in us to develop the fruits of righteousness through your spirit that dwells within us, so your efforts are multiplied, and your power is shown to those in our neighborhood and around the world! Make our good works and your love and faithfulness become the talk of the world's media outlets and at the watercoolers, until all other things become boring and useless. Help us, as you did Job in his time of trial. To live a life worthy of our calling, and bless us so we are able to complete all you have called us to do, in Jesus' name, amen.

FOR DEEPER STUDY:

Deuteronomy 5 • Matthew 25 • Ephesians 5 • Philippians 1 • 2 Peter 1

J. Sharing in the Resurrection

Read Isaiah 58:12 – 14

Read Matthew 25: 1 – 5

Read Romans 8: 28 – 30

> 1 CORINTHIANS 15: 50 - 53
>
> *I declare to you, brothers and sisters, that flesh and blood cannot inherit the kingdom of God, nor does the perishable inherit the imperishable.*

Prayer

Father, help us to be faithful, moving in step with your Spirit, you leading us to battle and tear down spiritual strongholds and hurtful ideals, and building dwellings, upon the rock that cannot be moved! Grant us willing hearts to give shelter to all who seek to be with you, making ready your people for the day of your return. May we be wise and not foolish in all we think and do; remembering that your will and ways are flawless, and you are perfect, calling us to become pure in Spirit, heart, and mind. Amen.

FOR DEEPER STUDY:

Isaiah 26, 58 • Matthew 25 • Romans 8 • 1 Corinthians 15

PART 5

WORSHIP

(The believer's life)

Psalm 150 • John 3: 10 - 15 • 1 John 3: 19 – 24

JOHN 4: 23

Yet, a time is coming and has now come when the true worshipers will worship the Father in the Spirit and in truth, for they are the kind of worshipers the Father seeks.

Prayer

Father, let us experience the joy of relationship with you! To be held, to be told, you are mine and I love you. We want our lives to mean something, and wish good things for our families, neighbors, coworkers, and friends. But sin has clouded people's sight, and many distractions abound. Less of the flesh, more of the spirit, less doubt, more faith, less complaining, more gratitude. Show us that we are surrounded by your arms, by thousands of angels, ready to minister and war, and souls in need of Jesus. Let our worship raise you up and draw all mankind to you. Amen.

FOR DEEPER STUDY:

Psalm 150 • John 3, 4 • 1 John 3

CHAPTER 17

NEW CREATIONS

(Into the temple of God)

2 Corinthians 5 • Galatians 6 • Colossians 2

So, we all get up every morning, and go to school or work, what do we do that reminds us that we are new creations? Many of us seem to be pigeon-holed by societies norms, and expectations. I will remind every believer that in Christ Jesus, each one of us has been crucified, and our receipt of the Holy Spirit means we are new creations.

Our morning prayer should be to thank God for being recreated, and ask the Spirit to work on us to remake us in God's image, giving us challenges, opportunities, and sacrifices to make that lift Jesus' name, and show grace and love in our lives to everyone He has us meet! Let the joy of being redeemed and reconciled to God in Christ Jesus give you peace and joy that is immeasurable.

GALATIANS 6: 8

For he who sows to his flesh will of the flesh reap corruption, but he who sows to the Spirit will of the Spirit reap everlasting life.

When Jesus said, "it is finished." The flesh went to the grave with Him, and we were forgiven, one time forever. And Jesus single-handedly defeated the fallen angels, and made their plans fall like lightening from heaven.

A. Made in God's Image

Read Genesis 1: 26 – 28

Read 2 Corinthians 5: 16 – 19

Read Colossians 1: 14 – 18

REVELATION 3: 12

He who overcomes, I will make him a pillar in the temple of My God, and he shall go out no more. I will write on him the name of My God and the name of the city of My God, the New Jerusalem, which comes down out of heaven from My God. And I will write on him My new name.

Prayer

We have crucified the flesh within, and agree in prayer to bind all agreements past, present, or future of anyone to these idols, and loose your love, blessing, grace, and compassion on mankind. Reconcile us, we pray to you, so we may commune with you once again. Give us that power to open the eyes of the blind to see how powers and principalities influence our world. Purify our hearts, minds, and souls, redeem the time, and make us fearless as we speak your truth into our world. Amen.

FOR DEEPER STUDY:

Genesis 1 • Exodus 20 • 2 Corinthians 5 • Colossians 1 • Revelation 3

B. Dead to Sin, Risen to Life

Read Psalm 20: 4 – 8

Read Romans 6: 10 – 14

Read Revelation 1: 4 – 6

ISAIAH 40: 31

But those who wait on the Lord Shall renew their strength; They shall mount up with wings like eagles. They shall run and not be weary. They shall walk and not faint.

Prayer

Father, we thank you that we're not robots, but you made us with a will. May our hearts choose wisely and rejoice in your free gift to us through Christ Jesus. May we never again trust in the plans of man. Make us clean by the water of baptism, taking hold of the Spirit of almighty God, to lead, guide, protect, and move us, showering us with blessing and giving us abiding peace. When old habits temptations, or ideas show themselves, remove our rough edges, and make us into your image, giving us abilities that seem Supernatural, because we are children of our God and maker. We will have power to do His will.

FOR DEEPER STUDY:

Psalm 20 • Isaiah 40 • Romans 6 • Revelation 1

C. Hidden in Christ

Read Psalm 61: 3 – 5

Read 1 Corinthians 15: 53 – 37

Read Colossians 3: 1 – 4

HEBREWS 9: 14

how much more shall the blood of Christ, who through the eternal Spirit offered Himself without spot to God, cleanse your conscience from dead works to serve the living God?

Prayer

Father, let us come to you for shelter, refuge, and peace. Thank you that you love us so much that you provided the perfect sacrifice for our sin, and His blood will cover all our sins. So too, you cover our mortality with everlasting life, and forgive us our sins. Jesus said wherever our treasure is there too will our hearts be. May our hearts never be divided, or seeking more as if you are not enough. Keep our hearts, minds, and souls on you. May we daily as with one voice say you are my God and King!

FOR DEEPER STUDY:

Psalm 61 • Matthew 6 • 1 Corinthians 15
• Colossians 3 • Hebrews 9

D. Destroying & Rebuilding

Read Exodus 34: 11 – 14

Read Isaiah 58: 11 – 13

Read 2 Corinthians 10: 3 – 6

2 CHRONICLES 7: 14

if My people who are called by My name will humble themselves, and pray and seek My face, and turn from their wicked ways, then I will hear from heaven, and will forgive their sin and heal their land.

Prayer

Father, we ask you not to take away our pains, struggles, and anguish, instead we ask for obedient, faithful, and courageous hearts that will obey you, knowing that your Son paid the ultimate price, but showed us the way to you! Help us to do as Isaiah and Haggai prophesied, and rebuild the body, the temple of the Lord. Give us hearts to reach all who will dedicate their life to show they love like you love us! Cover us with the armor Paul spoke of in Ephesians, and help us in prayer to agree to bind evil and destroy arguments against you. Give us humble hearts we pray, Amen.

FOR DEEPER STUDY:

Exodus 34 • 2 Chronicles 7 • Isaiah 58 • 2 Corinthians 10

E. Descended From Abraham

Read Genesis 17: 6 – 8

Read Matthew 2: 5 – 7

Read Galatians 3: 27 – 29

COLOSSIANS 3: 17

And whatever you do in word or deed, do all in the name of the Lord Jesus, giving thanks to God the Father through Him.

Prayer

Father, we know we are made in your image, and even though you sent Jesus to die in our place, grant that we might see the extent of your love in this life, displayed through our lives. As the Israelites were in Canaan, so we are in this world, and like the saints before us, we long for the life to come, but we know that you are the reward that nothing on earth can equal. We know that many are the nations that are descended from Abraham, but you set the record straight, clarifying that all who believe in your son, are children of Abraham. May word and deeds show we are descended from you! Amen.

FOR DEEPER STUDY:

Genesis 17 • Matthew 2 • Galatians 3 • Colossians 3

F. Grafted In & Producing

Read Romans 11: 22 – 24

Read Galatians 5: 22 – 26

Read Hebrews 6: 6 – 8

> PROVERBS 18: 21 - 22
>
> *Death and life are in the power of the tongue, and those who love it will eat its fruit.*

Prayer

Father, we are surprised by your approach in grafting in those who decide to trust and obey, and cutting out those who will not, we thank you for seeing our potential when we could not. Make our hearts brim with the fruits of the Spirit, so that people might see it this as more delightful than what the earth offers. Make it so fruitful in the lives of your people that it is never out of season, and brings hope and strength to those who are oppressed, doubtful, and in distress. Help us to cultivate our gift, fanning into flame the giftings you have given through your Holy Spirit. Let all who see and hear have no doubts. Amen.

FOR DEEPER STUDY:

Proverbs 18 • Romans 11 • Galatians 5 • Hebrews 6

G. Word Fills the Earth

Read Psalm 33: 6 – 9

Read Psalm 107: 19 – 22

Read Hebrews 1: 1 – 4

PSALM 18: 30

As for God, His way is perfect; The word of the Lord is proven; He is a shield to all who trust in Him.

Prayer

Thanksgiving and rejoicing, that we have a loving and perfect God, who can identify with our weaknesses and obstacles because of the life and death of his son, Jesus Christ. We see your word displayed from our vantage point on earth to the galaxies above and beyond. Grant us awestruck, delighted, and content hearts, to push aside sinful pursuits, embrace you, and show our world that nothing is better or more important than loving you and one another. Send help speedily when needed, and give rest as needed so we will be refreshed, and encouraged. Give us something that makes the world ask, how? This we ask in Jesus' name, amen.

FOR DEEPER STUDY:

Psalm 19, 33, 107 • Ecclesiastes 3 • Hebrews 1

H. Growing As Disciples

Read Matthew 9: 35 – 37

Read 1 Corinthians 9: 24 – 27

Read Hebrews 12: 5 – 9

> 1 CORINTHIANS 3: 7
>
> *So, then neither he who plants is anything, nor he who waters, but God who gives the increase.*

Prayer

Father, let us live as ambassadors of you, and doing as Jesus did, preaching the good news, healing hurts, and showing them a better way. Let us not ask the potter, "why was I made this way?" instead let us ask, "how best can I be used to give glory and honor to you?" This is our life's work as disciples. Give us inquiring, soft, and child-like hearts and faith to your methods, and the people you put in our path, for we are rough rocks that you are making into diamonds. May we likewise see this as necessary for our eternal purpose, and give thanks that you have chosen us. Let pride be far from us, for when we are able to see your plans for others, and make us work together, then true leaders are realized! Amen.

FOR DEEPER STUDY:

Matthew 9 • 1 Corinthians 3, 9 • Hebrews 12

I. Spiritual Salt, Fruit & Light

Read Matthew 5: 13 – 16

Read Galatians 5: 22 – 25

Read Ephesians 5: 8 – 11

JOHN 8: 12

Then Jesus spoke to them again, saying, "I am the light of the world. He whofollows Me shall not walk in darkness, but have the light of life."

Prayer

Father, thank you for giving us everything necessary to live, and blessing us with abilities to enjoy this life. Help us to be just as essential as salt, fruit, and light in the lives of all those around us. May we sustain people with flavor, delight, and provide light that leads to life everlasting. Maximize our light in every way so that all may be attracted to it like a moth to a flame. With all the fruits that were available in the garden, we chose wrongly, but may we show people there is better fruit to enjoy, now and forever, without consequences, your Spirit giving it life. As your light shows forth may more be drawn to that life, following it all the way to life anew, in Jesus, Amen.

FOR DEEPER STUDY:

Matthew 5 • John 8 • Galatians 5 • Ephesians 5

J. Meditate on These Things

Read Joshua 1: 7 - 9

Read Psalms 119: 9 - 16

Read Philippians 4: 6 - 9

> 1 TIMOTHY 4: 16
>
> *Take heed to yourself and to the doctrine. Continue in them, for in doing this you will save both yourself and those who hear you.*

Prayer

Father, help our minds and hearts be stayed on you. Let nothing on this earth or any of its sinful passions or trappings or ideals take your place. Keep us in your hand, and your hand and Spirit guiding us, with your word leading us forward. Amplify your word more than any idea, impulse, or impression that excites and interests us, and lead us to practical ways to make your word real in our lives. May we delight in keeping your word, and rise on wings, like eagles as Isaiah says. Let nothing slow us or stop us, and let us give to you all things that make us anxious or depressed. Amen.

FOR DEEPER STUDY:

Joshua 1 • Psalm 119 • Philippians 4 • 1 Timothy 4

CHAPTER 18

OVERFLOWING

(Filling the world)

Proverbs 3 • 2 Corinthians 9 • Colossians 2

While writing these books, I've been looking at all the programs so called experts and gurus have for marketing, and some commercials have come up asking if I want to make real income as a Christian and eventually be financially independent. Some people may think this crazy, after all, to serve God and man, and wages for work is fair. But God isn't satisfied with us giving a little bit of ourselves to Him, and He is willing to give us everything! Jesus proved this on the cross!

Disciplined so we stay in God's will, pruned so we will be more abundant in producing fruit, becoming the delight of God. From Shepherd, to warrior, to hunted, to king, The story of David seems to cover this well. Some have pointed out that David was far from perfect, but God loved him, and he always kept accounts short. This included hit affair with Bathsheba, God sent Nathan to confront him, and there were consequences, but there was also forgiveness.

COLOSSIANS 2: 2 - 4

My goal is that they may be encouraged in heart and united in love, so that they may have the full riches of complete understanding, in order that they may know the mystery of God, namely, Christ, in whom are hidden all the treasures of wisdom and knowledge. I tell you this so that no one may deceive you by fine-sounding arguments.

Sowing and reaping are not just a matter of farming, but in the Christian life, spreading or our talents, time, and funds, and how much time, effort, and time is spent in this activity is seen and blessed by God.

A. By the Lord's Spirit & By His Design

Read Isaiah 26: 8 – 10

Read Zechariah 4: 3 – 7

Read Matthew 3: 10 – 12

EPHESIANS 2: 7

That in the ages to come He might show the exceeding riches of His grace in His kindness toward us in Christ Jesus.

Prayer

Father, may our hearts desire you, and your love for humanity that you have created. May we offer ourselves as instruments of your Spirit, to do great things, to produce works in the lives of others that only you could do through prophets, priest, and kings before the death and resurrection of Jesus. Though many yearn to be baptized for repentance of sin, may all receive the free gift of Your Holy Spirit, filling us to overflowing, leaving is no room for sin, or its lusts to ever come back. May your gifts of grace reach to heaven. Amen.

FOR DEEPER STUDY:

Isaiah 26 • Zechariah 4 • Matthew 3 • Ephesians 2

B. Divine Power

Read Psalm 26: 1 – 8

Read Acts 17: 26 – 30

Read 2 Corinthians 10: 14 – 18

2 PETER 1: 3

...as His divine power has given to us all things that pertain to life and godliness, through the knowledge of Him who called us by glory and virtue.

Prayer

In a world of war, slavery, child labor, devoid of human rights, stand up for your people, whom you have created in your image, and judge those who have forgotten that they are but dirt, and to dirt we all return! Help us also to stand for the innocent, the ridiculed, the oppressed, the missing, and murdered. When we cannot, let our prayers rise commanding your angels to intervene. Let us remember that to some we minister, with others we contend, in the faith and in terms of moral obligation, because we are followers of Christ. Lead us to a godly life, in all we do. Amen.

FOR DEEPER STUDY:

Psalm 26 • Acts 17 • 2 Corinthians 10 • 2 Peter 1

C. God the Kingdom Grower

Read Mark 4: 30 - 32

Read Ephesians 2: 19 – 22

Read Colossians 2: 16 – 19

EPHESIANS 4: 16

from whom the whole body, joined and knit together by what every joint supplies, according to the effective working by which every part does its share, causes growth of the body for the edifying of itself in love.

Prayer

Father, we know that Jesus used the earthly examples of plants, stones, and the laws and ideas of man, but the kingdom of God is one that's neither earthly nor anything that could be contrived by man. Abraham was told to count the sand of the seashore if he could and was told his offspring would equal that. May each day our faith, love and grace grow, amidst the pain, suffering, build your kingdom, with us, with your Spirit as the mortar holding us together. May your word feed us daily, building our nourishment and strength, until we are complete. Amen.

FOR DEEPER STUDY:

Mark 4 • Ephesians 2, 4 • Colossians 2

D. Judging Nations & Angels

Read Joel 3: 1 – 3

Read Matthew 25: 34 – 36

Revelation 11: 16 – 19

> 1 CORINTHIANS 6: 2
>
> *Do you not know that the saints will judge the world? And if the world will be judged by you, are you unworthy to judge the smallest matters?*

Prayer

Father, now I lay me down to sleep, bless those who've lost all and weep, give time to all who seek your face, judge those whose hatred erases all grace. Face down the tyrants, the deceivers, and all who make deals with the fallen, remind them their ends will come, like Hitler and Stalin. As the Assyrians did to Israel, so they do now. Help us inherit the earth, we humbly bow; asking in faith, to serve and lead the world with your word to satisfy and feed. The powers of sin and hell subdued, let our conduct never be rude. Courage and strength we pray, judgment on those who kill for play. (Author Unknown) Amen.

FOR DEEPER STUDY:

Joel 3 • Matthew 25 • 1 Corinthians 6 • Revelation 11

E. On Fire for Him

Read Acts 2: 1 – 4

Read 2 Corinthians 9: 1 – 3

Read Hebrews 10: 23 – 25

ROMANS 8: 19

For the earnest expectation of the creation eagerly waits for the revealing of the sons of God.

Prayer

Father, thank you for sending your Holy Spirit, help us to corporately call for your Spirit to lead and guide our lives, making baptism the moment that all will die to self and receive the Spirit. We long for the opportunity to live in the Spirit, and show your power to the world; bringing heaven to earth, and lifting the veil on you and life everlasting. Like a fire burning out of control, make us burn with your power to please you and save souls. Grant that our message and deeds may spread faster and further than fire, or make petrol to fuel it. Make people also see, and know that we believe, follow, and live, for you. Amen.

FOR DEEPER STUDY:

Acts 2 • Romans 8 • 2 Corinthians 9 • Hebrews 10

F. Feeding on the Word

Read Deuteronomy 28: 13 – 15

Read Psalm 119: 57 – 64

Read 2 Timothy 1: 8 – 10

JOB 23: 12

I have not departed from the commandment of His lips; I have treasured the words of His mouth More than my necessary food.

Prayer

Your promise that if we put you above everything else in life, and have no other gods, you will take us above our troubles. You are our reward, treasure, and portion, we rejoice for all you have done and will do in our lives, and through us. Break the binds of the enemy due to the sins and agreements of our past. Shatter the chains to pieces and grant us joy, peace and grace. Give us a swelling and overflowing with joy to speak of the good news of what you have done, and let this message touch a thousand people when we speak. There is urgency to give to all this good news, like an appetite for food.

FOR DEEPER STUDY:

Deuteron. 28 • Job 23 • Psalm 119 • 2 Timothy 1

G. Shining the Light of life

Read John 3: 18 – 21

Read Ephesians 5: 10 – 14

Read 2 Timothy 1: 8 – 10

MATTHEW 5: 16

Let your light so shine before men, that they may see your good works and glorify your Father in heaven.

Prayer

Thank you for sending your son as a light in the world, help us to be light bearers, and examples of your love and authority to all who are in hiding or denial. Your light has shown us a better life awaits; we will pass this message to all who will listen, and bear witness so all the world will see the light. In a world of doubt and darkness, may your truth and light give truth, life, and purpose. This is what you had in mind all along, and were thankful you have given this gift to us, to have and to share. Make us bright as lighthouses, with you to save and guide us all. Amen.

FOR DEEPER STUDY:

Matthew 5 • John 3 • Ephesians 5 • 2 Timothy 1

H. Opening His Treasury, Blessing

Read Deuteronomy 28: 1 – 4

Read Malachi 3: 9 – 11

Read Romans 15: 12 – 14

> JAMES 1: 17
>
> *Every good gift and every perfect gift is from above, and comes down from the Father of lights, with whom there is no variation or shadow of turning.*

Prayer

His death and resurrection opened the gates of heaven to all who believe and receive Him. Moses' blessing from you gave the Israelites everything for living in this world you have given us. We acknowledge our death to sin and ask for your blessings on our new lives in Christ, grant us hearts of thanksgiving, gratitude, and compassion that gives as graciously as you have given to us. Open the floodgates of Heaven and bless us now so we may do all that you require, rebuke the devourer, and give us enough. Make us confident in speaking truth to all who will listen, and may our acts and words magnify you and your son, all thanks be to you.

FOR DEEPER STUDY:

Deuteronomy 28 • Malachi 3 • Romans 15 • James 1

I. Laying Up Treasures in Heaven

Read Matthew 6: 19 – 21

Read Matthew 19: 28 – 30

Read Luke 6: 20 – 23

ISAIAH 51: 6

Lift up your eyes to the heavens, and look on the earth beneath. For the heavens will vanish away like smoke, The earth will grow old like a garment, and those who dwell in it will die in like manner; But My salvation will be forever, And My righteousness will not be abolished.

Prayer

Father, help us! In our world, people trade each other for favors, power, for money, or things unmentionable. Help us to see that the most important things in life aren't things at all. Grant us a passion to know your will and ways, to treasure you, your words, and the people around us, laying them up as treasures in heaven, as Jesus taught. Remind us that those who have left behind the loves of the sin nature will inherit salvation of their souls and eternal life, and 100 times more of everything. May both you and the people around us call us blessed. In Jesus' name, Amen.

FOR DEEPER STUDY:

Isaiah 51 • Matthew 6, 19 • Luke 6

J. Rejoice & Pray Continually

Read Psalm 35: 26 – 28

Read 2 Timothy 1: 3 – 5

Read 1 Thessalonians 5: 16 – 22

1 PETER 5: 7

Casting all your cares upon Him, for He cares for you.

Prayer

Father, give us clarity of mind to not fall for their smoke and mirrors, and instead have our minds on you making you bigger than any man-made issue, law, or conflict. Make us courageous in preaching the gospel, and shameless in loving our fellow man and woman in Christ, and leading them to the truth, encouraging their faith. As we exercise bed time justice in our prayers to you, may we be as fiery as David was in the Psalms, and as concerned as Jesus for all. Grant that your Spirit within us would not let our minds be silent at prayer time, help us unload all, and sleep peacefully. Amen.

FOR DEEPER STUDY:

Psalm 35 • 2 Timothy 1 • 1 Thessalonians 5 • 1 Peter 5

CHAPTER 19

CONFIDENT

(Persevere in faith)

1 Samuel 15 • Psalm 71 • 2 Corinthians 3

There are many confident persons on the world stage. Russian President Putin has pushed his armed forces into Ukraine in an act of war, Ukranian President Zelenskyy says the people of Ukraine will fight to the end to defend it. The war has waged about a year and three weeks, and we wonder how long either side can continue in this conflict. Both remain confident.

Many times, in the old-testament we read that countries put confidence in kings, armies, chariots, iron, and armies. The Philistines put their confidence in a giant named Goliath. A 16-year-old boy with a slingshot and stone killed him. Saul moved rebelliously in his own power, then sacrificed some of the plunder to appease God because he didn't listen to the command to wait for a blessing from Samuel, and was rejected as king of Israel.

If you look at arts, music, entertainment, news, and political ideologies, and approaches to education, and religion, there is a movement whose agenda is to "dumb down" the people. Indeed, even as a society, no one is allowed to be trusting, vulnerable, or gracious. In an effort to prevent spread of airborne illnesses were wearing masks. The information age has governments and big business mining our browsing on the net, so we veil our activities.

The life we live proves God has removed His veil so we may see Him clearly. The veil in the temple to the Holy of Holies was torn in two from top to bottom, giving mankind access to the throne room of heaven. This is true confidence that we have what we ask for, and His Spirit is our guarantee that "we can do all things through Jesus who strengthens us.

A. No Other Gods/Way

Read Exodus 23: 10 – 13

Read Deuteronomy 13: 12 – 16

Read Isaiah 45: 18 – 21

JOHN 14: 6

Jesus said to him, "I am the way, the truth, and the life. No one comes to the Father except through Me.

Prayer

Let us rejoice, Father, in your sabbath rest! You rested from creation, and it was good. You call on us to follow your commandments with our heart, soul, and strength, work hard, but count on you for sustenance and wages. In return, you call us to show that we are different. Our world struggles to gather all they can, but they suffer and do not see that their days ahead are few and full of strife. Let us be open books, showing you are true, and good, and steadfast, a loving compassionate and giving Father, and the only one that can Save us all, because of the price Jesus paid on the cross. May everyone on earth say, there is but one way to heaven. Amen.

FOR DEEPER STUDY:

Exodus 23 • Deuteronomy 13 • Isaiah 45 • John 14

B. Ask Without Doubting

Read Romans 8: 22 - 25

Read James 1: 2 – 8

Read 1 Peter 1: 6 – 8

JOHN 1: 12

But as many as received Him, to them He gave the right to become children of God, to those who believe in His name.

Prayer

Father, grant us revelation in Spirit of all you want us to do. Encourage us to live a life that lifts your name, and gives new life to all who we reach with the gospel message. Be with us when we face trials, and give us strength, so that all may see you working powerfully within and alongside us. Let us recite the serenity prayer if it helps, and let us hold on to the faith with both hands, not willing to let go, whatever happens! Grant that our faith, hope, and love outshines this world in which we live, that when everything comes to an end and we see you face to face, we may have joy that words cannot convey, embracing as at a family reunion.

FOR DEEPER STUDY:

John 1 • Romans 8 • James 1 • 1 Peter 1

C. Refuge & Rest Abiding in His Presence

Read 2 Samuel 22: 44 – 50

Read Psalm 91: 1 – 4

Read John 15: 5 – 8

1 THESSALONIANS 2: 19

For what is our hope, or joy, or crown of rejoicing? Is it not even you in the presence of our Lord Jesus Christ at His coming?

Prayer

Father, thank you for righting the wrong of Adam and Eve in Eden. May we choose to abide with you in Spirit. This is life, and the opportunity to commune with you once again. No ideas or lies of our world compare to your shelter, our support that never will fade. In life, allow us time to abide in the refuge of your presence, sheltered from all that assails us, and the oppressive forces of darkness. Deliver us, we pray, from evil schemes and plans that would threaten to stop your work, or to destroy us. Refresh us when we become weary, and remind us that after all is done, we will abide with you, forever. Keep us focused on doing your will. This we ask in Jesus' name, amen.

FOR DEEPER STUDY:

2 Samuel 22 • Psalm 91 • Acts 3 • 1 Thessalonians 2

D. Hold On, Press In, Persevere

Read Philippians 3: 8 – 14

Read Hebrews 10: 19 – 24

Read Revelation 3: 8 – 11

PROVERBS 3: 6

In all your ways acknowledge Him, And He shall direct your paths. direct your paths.

Prayer

Father, nothing compares to faith in you, and honor that comes from you. Help us pass every blessing every enticement on earth for the life that awaits us. Give us confidence to throw open the gates of heaven and yell, "Daddy, I'm home and I am ready to meet you, and take hold of the new life you have prepared for me! Thank you for my baptism, which cleansed me from a sinful shameful conscience, and give me a heart to stir up the Spirit of all around me." Let our response be one that leaves no room for doubt, in the disobedient and the fallen. We will persevere until the day of your coming. In Jesus' name, amen.

FOR DEEPER STUDY:

Proverbs 3 • Philippians 3 • Hebrews 10 • Revelation 3

E. Ever Present Father

Read Psalm 139: 7 – 12

Read Ezekiel 9: 8 – 11

Read Hebrews 13: 4 – 9

2 CORINTHIANS 5: 8

We are confident, yes, well pleased rather to be absent from the body and to be present with the Lord

Prayer

Thank you, Father, that you will never leave or forsake us. We echo David, who asked, "What is man that you are mindful of him?" And you are, your word shows us just how much you love us, and there can be no other response but to love you back! Nothing shall ever separate us from you, we are together, forever! "I'm forgiven, because he was forsaken, I'm accepted, he was condemned!" Continue to be our helper to the end of our days, giving us loving and wise hearts that help the poor, forgive sinners, and obey rulers, so no one can say bad about us. May we too be present with you. Amen.

FOR DEEPER STUDY:

Psalm 139 • Ezekiel 9 • Hebrews 13 • 2 Corinthians 5

F. Unchanging Love

Read John 15: 9 – 15

Read Hebrews 10: 32 – 36

Read James 1: 12 – 18

ECCLESIASTES 3: 10 - 12

He has made everything beautiful in its time. Also, He has put eternity in their hearts, except that no one can find out the work that God does from beginning to end.

Prayer

Father, we know that you do not change, and your agenda has never changed, you want to give the opportunity for your word to reach all the ends of the earth, so that all that is left is to choose sides. All who choose to be your children, will be, and will act as such, the rest will be children of Satan, and follow him. Give us strength to endure and overcome, so that we will receive the crown of life, because we have used every gift you have given us to show we are legitimate children, and that you love us. We accept your love, and the opportunity to live an eternity of love and joy and peace in relationship with you. Amen.

FOR DEEPER STUDY:

Ecclesiastes 3 • John 15 • James 1 • Hebrews 10

G. Loving, Submissive Sacrifice

Read Micah 6: 6 – 9

Read Romans 12: 1 – 8

Read Hebrews 13: 10 – 17

1 PETER 2: 5

... you also, as living stones, are being built up a spiritual house, a holy priesthood, to offer up spiritual sacrifices acceptable to God through Jesus Christ.

Prayer

Father, may we grow daily in our curiosity of you, and what it means to live in Spirit, as we tarry in this dying body and world, and see the consequences of mankind's sins, were tired! We dedicate our lives to you, our families, friends, and communities, to becoming your children, and showing the world a better way to live, remind us who we are and whose we are, and help us to move united in belief, and in love, showing your power to a world of lost souls. Keep our souls and minds in loving one another, and on the life that is to come, building your kingdom, each of us using the gifts you have given us. So that all may show themselves to be your children.

FOR DEEPER STUDY:

Micah 6 • Romans 12 • Hebrews 13 • 1 Peter 2

H. Wolves at the Door

Read Ezekiel 22: 26 – 30

Read Matthew 10: 16 – 20

Read 1 Peter 5: 6 – 11

PSALM 23: 4

Yea, though I walk through the valley of the shadow of death, I will fear no evil; For You are with me; Your rod and Your staff, they comfort me.

Prayer

Father, grant that we would not only honor your works and your holy day, but also remain pure, not mixing your word with worldly ideas. Help us to beware of wolves, in society, government, and corporations. Make the works of evil of no result, and may the profits of the greedy and hateful end up in the hands of the impoverished. Make us strong when we fall to leaders of evil, trusting that you will speak through us, by the power of the Spirit. Give us wisdom to know when to avoid situations and when to engage the enemy, knowing that you are in control. Make us a victory dinner while in the company of our enemies. Amen.

FOR DEEPER STUDY:

Psalm 23 • Ezekiel 22 • Matthew 10 • 1 Peter 5

I. Armed for Daily Combat

Read Acts 1: 4 – 8

Read Ephesians 6: 10 – 13

Read Hebrews 4: 11 – 16

JAMES 1: 4

But let patience have its perfect work, that you may be perfect and complete, lacking nothing.

Prayer

Father, help us meditate on it, and learn to communicate with you. May we, like the disciples discover the power of unity, and corporate prayer, in groups and in your church, to receive the Holy Spirit, and move as you lead us. Clothe us in the Spiritual armor, so that we will be safe from the attacks of our enemy, and move to tear down strongholds, in individuals and groups, and kingdoms, knowing that everything we do on earth is being done in heaven. Let nothing steal our crown or thunder, as we continue in your will and ways, and make us understand that all that happens is for good because we trust in you to make it end well for one and all. Amen.

FOR DEEPER STUDY:

Acts 1 • Ephesians 6 • Hebrews 4 • James 1

J. Footprints in the Sand

Read Psalm 4: 4 – 8

Read 1 Peter 3: 13 – 17

Read 1 Peter 5: 5 – 7

ISAIAH 41: 10

Fear not, for I am with you; Be not dismayed, for I am your God. I will strengthen you. Yes, I will help you, I will uphold you with My righteous right hand.

Prayer

Father, when the pain, struggle, and trials seem to overwhelm, teach us the joy of surrender to you! The cross and the sacrifice of Jesus was enough for you to accepts us, so show us how to let go, of anger, injustice, oppression, sin, greeds, lusts, and all that clouds hearts and minds, and know that you have it in your control. Take our worries, and anxieties when we cast them on you, as Peter suggests. Show us that it is you who carries us if we should run out of strength. You promised to lift us up with your right hand. May all see, and put their faith and hope in you. In Jesus name, amen.

FOR DEEPER STUDY:

Psalm 4 • Isaiah 41 • 1 Peter 3, 5

CHAPTER 20

AUTHORITY

(Your will be done)

Romans 8 • Hebrews 9 • Revelation 22

Has anyone ever heard of Mind search? I know God formed me in the womb. But God also searches our hearts and minds. He is keenly aware of our plans, our motives, and He has predestined our outcomes! This has been a source of controversy in the church, but the only thing we can conclude is God's will be done, on earth as it is in heaven!

Because we believe in His son, and decided to follow Him, God has redeemed us and reconciled us to Himself, that we should become His children! Christ Jesus is our High priest, He was the perfect sacrifice, and dwells in the heavenly tabernacle, which is both high above, and within us, by the power of the Holy Spirit. Earthly sacrifices were continual, Jesus was perfect and his one-time sacrifice made us eternally clean and adopted as children.

HEBREWS 9: 14, 15

How much more, then, will the blood of Christ, who through the eternal Spirit offered himself unblemished to God, cleanse our consciences from acts that lead to death, so that we may serve the living God! For this reason, Christ is the mediator of a new covenant, that those who are called may receive the promised eternal inheritance—now that he has died as a ransom to set them free from the sins committed under the first covenant.

A day is coming when Jesus will return to punish the fallen angels and all who follow them and their acts of evil, oppression, resulting in death. They will be sent to a place of eternal pain and torment, but those who repent will join God and Jesus as family!

A. Limited, Eternal Time Offers

Read Matthew 24: 36 – 39

Read 1 Corinthians 2: 9 – 12

Read 1 Corinthians 6: 1 – 3

> 1 CORINTHIANS 15: 50
>
> *Now, this I say, brethren, that flesh and blood cannot inherit the kingdom of God; nor does corruption inherit in corruption.*

Prayer

Father, fill us with your Spirit, overwhelmed by your love, and willing to share with all who will listen, pleading that they receive this limited time offer. The times of Noah are upon us, when people do what they want, but Jesus's return is sure. Grant us hearts to go to the ends of the earth, and work miracles like none have seen before so others may plainly see we are your children, and give you praise. As the fields are ready, may we all work your grace into situations, circumstances, and show forth your Spirit, so all know, that only by the Spirit can we inherit your kingdom, and escape damnation.

FOR DEEPER STUDY:

Matthew 24 • 1 Corinthians 2, 6, 15

B. Rewards & Spoils

Read Psalm 19: 7 – 11

Read Matthew 5: 3 – 12

Read Revelation 11: 15 – 18

REVELATION 21: 4

And God will wipe away every tear from their eyes; there shall be no more death, nor sorrow, nor crying. There shall be no more pain, for the former things have passed away.

Prayer

Father, some of us will not get to grow old in our faith life, but we hope to never wonder what it was like before we believed! Help us to take in your word and ways as plants take in sunshine, rejoicing in how it makes things clearer and clearer. May we value you and your word more than the riches of earth. Bless all who are true, and may we all work to eagerly see the day when we will meet our maker. For some of us, meeting you is reward enough, some will receive their friends and families, and the admiration and thanks of all who shared the gospel message, and gave of their gifts, and blessed others as you have blessed us. Life everlasting will be exciting, and different, I cannot wait. Amen.

FOR DEEPER STUDY:

Psalm 19 • Matthew 5 • Revelation 11, 21

C. Battle Won on Calvary

Read 1 Corinthians 15: 20 – 28

Read Ephesians 4: 11 – 16

Read Hebrews 10: 5 – 10

> JOHN 19
>
> *So, when Jesus had received the sour wine, He said, "It is finished!" And bowing His head, He gave up His spirit.*

Prayer

Thank you for your law, to convict our hearts of sin, and Your word, for telling us the Gospel story of Jesus' life and death and sacrifice on the cross. Thank you also for giving your disciples, with a pattern to follow, so we too may become like Jesus, having a heart to obey the Father, trust your Spirit, and to lie as Jesus did! We long for our enemies to be put under foot, but know the war is already won, we just need to unite and follow. Make us courageous, using our gifts to their full potential, giving glory to you. Jesus said, we would do greater things than He did, making the world turn their attention back to a caring, loving, and all-powerful God. When life is over, may we, like Jesus, look upon the world without regret saying, it is finished.

FOR DEEPER STUDY:

John 19 • 1 Corinthians 15 • Ephesians 4 • Hebrews 10

D. A Royal Priesthood

Read Hebrews 4: 14 – 16

Read Hebrews 8: 1 – 6

Read 1 Peter 2: 5 – 10

PSALM 51: 10

The sacrifices of God are a broken spirit, A broken and a contrite heart— These, O God, You will not despise.

Prayer

Thank you, Father that you were not satisfied with just being our God, but sent your son Jesus, who lived among a sinful people, and felt the sting of sin, the temptation of Satan, but remained faithful. Grant us mercy, and forgive, giving us hearts filled to overflowing with love, leaving behind regret, hurts, and grudges, and instead forgiving our brothers and sisters as you have forgiven us. As Jesus has given a better covenant than in Moses' day, and a pattern for us to follow, may we daily give our lives in sacrifice to you, knowing that only by the blood of Jesus is our sacrifice accepted by you. May this daily act of obedience do on earth what is done in heaven, binding and losing the right things, and showing the world a better way, In Jesus' name, amen.

FOR DEEPER STUDY:

Psalm 51 • Hebrews 4, 8 • 1 Peter 2

E. Heart, Mind, & Strength

Read Joshua 24: 13 – 15

Read Matthew 6: 23 – 25

Read Colossians 3: 18 – 25

ISAIAH 50: 10

Who among you fears the Lord? Who obeys the voice of His Servant? Who walks in darkness And has no light? Let him trust in the name of the Lord And rely upon his God.

Prayer

I pray that we may never sit on the fence; for you call on your people to be hot or cold, because the Luke-warm will be spit out of your mouth. Grant us eyes filled with your loving kindness, mercy, and grace, so that we will not be deceived by riches or empty ideologies, or fill our lives with worry and forget about you. Give us humble and obedient hearts, not necessarily agreeing with the ideas of unwise leaders, but submitting to authority so that leaders know we follow you, and trust in your word, in Jesus' name, amen.

FOR DEEPER STUDY:

Joshua 24 • Isaiah 50 • Matthew 6 • Colossians 3

F. Fulfillment of the Law

Read Matthew 5: 17 - 20

Read Matthew 22: 34 - 40

Read Romans 13: 7 - 10

JAMES 2: 8

If you really fulfill the royal law according to the Scripture, "You shall love your neighbor as yourself," you do well;

Prayer

Father, your law makes perfect sense as the one theme that sums up the Holy Bible! Make us ready and willing to testify of your goodness and all you have done from beginning to end. Telling all that there is not one that has not broken the law, but that Jesus made it possible for forgiveness of sin and call us to repentance and righteousness in Christ Jesus. Let your word and ways permeate our being, so your Spirit may rule in our hearts, minds, mouths, and deeds, doing great things for you. Make us law abiding and peaceful among people of all nations, showing by our conduct that the law is our conscience. Help us to do all to fulfil your law, in our conduct, in our families, in our workplaces and communities, in Jesus' name, amen.

FOR DEEPER STUDY:

Matthew 5 • Matthew 22 • Romans 13 • James 2

G. Divine Weaponry

Read Psalm 34: 4 – 10

Read Matthew 26: 50 – 54

Read 2 Corinthians 10: 1 – 6

HEBREWS 4: 12

For the word of God is living and powerful, and sharper than any two-edged sword, piercing even to the division of soul and spirit, and of joints and marrow, and is a discerner of the thoughts and intents of the heart.

Prayer

Father, deliver your people, with your powerful words, help us to use them to bind and loose, to minister to others, and to call on your ministering and warring angels in times they are needed. We know, many times, Satan and his angels have been in heaven, and on earth, and many times they have fallen. Make us see that the enemy is before us and in you we will be victorious! Not by might or by strength, but by your spirit. Give us courage to break strongholds and make the mountains and valleys plain so that the way is clear for all to come, and repent, and be baptized, and receive you and join us in this fight. Amen.

FOR DEEPER STUDY:

Psalm 34 • Matthew 26 • 2 Corinthians 10 • Hebrews 4

H. Vows, Prayers, & Binding Agreements

Read Deuteronomy 23: 30 – 23

Read Matthew 18: 15 – 20

Read Philippians 4: 4 – 9

ISAIAH 56: 7

Even them I will bring to My holy mountain, and make them joyful in My house of prayer. Their burnt offerings and their sacrifices Will be accepted on My altar; For My house shall be called a house of prayer for all nations."

Prayer

Father, we are obligated by governments and chartered banks to pay rates and fees that seem like usury, make your people well off enough to extend grace to all who ask; showing we, like you, give good things to those that ask. Give us wisdom to know and do your will. Give us a mouth to speak when it is encouraging, joyful, gracious, wise, and exultant. Grant that your Spirit helps us forgiving, and showing another when they offend. Help us to remember that in the Lord's prayer, it says, "Your will be done, on earth as it is done in heaven." May our prayers to you rise continually in your house. Amen.

FOR DEEPER STUDY:

Deuteronomy 23 • Isaiah 56 • Matthew 18 • Philippians 4

I. Bankrupt, All-In, or Gaining Christ (losing all)

Read Proverbs 1: 10 – 19

Read Matthew 16: 24 – 27

Read Philippians 3: 7 – 11

1 PETER 5: 2

Shepherd the flock of God which is among you, serving as overseers, not by compulsion but willingly, not for dishonest gain, but eagerly.

Prayer

Father, quicken our hearts with the thought of living the adventure of following you wherever a life in Christ will take us! Instead of being as the world that wills to take advantage of each other for ill gotten gains, let us look at the opportunity to make others see a new life that is in fact heavenly, and loving, better than anything this world can achieve. Help us to have a "whatever it takes attitude," that allows us to see that if we lose our lives, we gain life in Christ. We have been promised a very great reward, even Christ himself will sit down and break bread with us. May we think on this when we suffer all kinds of things. Amen Lord.

FOR DEEPER STUDY:

Proverbs 1 • Matthew 16 • Philippians 3 • 1 Peter 5

J. Judging the Nations in Love

Read Psalm 103: 1 – 8

Read Matthew 24: 6 – 8

Read Revelation 8: 1 – 5

COLOSSIANS 3: 14

But above all these things, put on love, which is the bond of perfection.

Prayer

Father, in your judgments, you know you gave us life, and you determined its length. Keep our hearts tender as we ask you to avenge our enemies, help us to see that everything must work out for good for all who you have called and gifted. Even now, we are in awe of you, and how you see things playing out between nations and kingdoms, and yet, you know the conclusion before it begins. We long for this end, but we too are cheering for you to make clear the line between, and the things that define us from the fallen. Make us advocates for the oppressed, the anxious, the hopeless, and give us your eyes to see people as you do, and judge the evil works of the fallen. Keep us loving and open to sharing you with all who will listen. In Jesus' name, amen.

FOR DEEPER STUDY:

Psalm 103 • Matthew 24 • Colossians 3 • Revelation 8

ABOUT GFCA

Grounding for Christian action is a ministry, seeking to establish:

- Christ's clear direction and shining a light amidst chaos.
- Your purpose/place in this world, preparation for the next!
- Faith, Hope, and Love, where they're lacking in the world!
- Knowing that life in Him, begins the moment we believe.
- Offering THE answer to all who question the hope we have.

Proceeds will be used to seed a ministry, (G.F.C.A.) develop and share materials relevant to this book, and be shared with:

- Samaritans Purse (BGEA)
- Wycliffe Bible Translators
- Youth With a Mission
- Teen Ranch Ministries
- Focus on the Family
- Prison Fellowship Min.
- Bible Discovery TV
- Insights for Living
- Dalit Freedom Network
- Covenant House

Books include: *8 Kudos for All Ages, This Little Light of Mine*

A future podcast: Winning@thehumanrace – where discusses issues of healthcare, wellbeing, relationships, justice, equality, and the environment. "Welcome to the Winning@thehumanrace Podcast, where competition is meaningless, but finishing strong is the goal!"

Future video training programs include: Reaching your goals, and Live to your potential

These are being produced under the umbrella of "CHEPFORA Communications" (Create, Honor, Empower, Persuade, Forgive, Observe, Relate, Advocate)

ACKNOWLEDGMENTS

Many Thanks to Nelson Thomas and Zondervan, the makers of Biblegateway.com. Scriptures taken from The New King James (NKJV) and New International (NIV) versions of the Bible.

Also, to Philip Yancey, who has shared emails of encouragement and suggestions in getting started with this work. To Nadene Joy, and Patricia Lameroux whose input on my previous work, which will be used in future books, is greatly appreciated.

To Derek Y. and family for putting their faith and support for my work in action, and my church family, Grace Community, for their prayer support in this and subsequent projects.

To Ghost Writers Network and Virtual Creatives for editing and publishing, encouraging me to jump into the work of getting my book published and ready for sale. And working with me to select front and back cover artwork, type face, formatting, ISBN Numbers, and associated tax paperwork.

To Kindlepreneur and Paper Raven books for ideas on pricing and the use of keywords so people can find me To Kindle Direct Publishing for setting me up with a digital sales platform for my first book, and Ingram Spark for doing my print work for this book.

Lastly to my girlfriend Jessica for supporting me in patience and prayer in completing this project, and God, for giving me the vision and insight to commence this project.

ABOUT THE AUTHOR

Paul Damsma is a Human Services Professional. With experiences in Mental Illness, Palliative Care, Brain Trauma, Children's Aid, and work with First Nations. He lives in Red Lake, Ontario, Canada.

www.ingramcontent.com/pod-product-compliance
Ingram Content Group UK Ltd.
Pitfield, Milton Keynes, MK11 3LW, UK
UKHW020132250726
13967UKWH00002B/599

9 781959 608417